The Musician's Diary

Music can noble hints impart
Engender fury, kindle love;
With unsuspected eloquence can move,
And Manage all the man with secret art.
                                    Joseph Addison

A McAfee Music Publication
Belwin-Mills Publishing Corp.
Melville, N.Y. 11747
PRINTED IN U.S.A.

ISBN No. 0-89328-032-1

JANUARY

MARTIN LUTHER KING DAY: The third Sunday

JANUARY 1

EDWIN FRANKO GOLDMAN
(1878-1956), U.S. bandmaster,
founder of the Goldman Band,
b. Louisville, Ky.

I AM thankful to be permitted, in the beginning of a New Year, to repeat with all the force of which my mind is yet capable the lesson I have endeavored to teach through my past life, that this fair Tree Igdrasil of Human Art can only flourish when its dew is Affection; its air, Devotion; the rock of its roots, Patience; and its sunshine, God.   RUSKIN.

NEW YEAR'S DAY

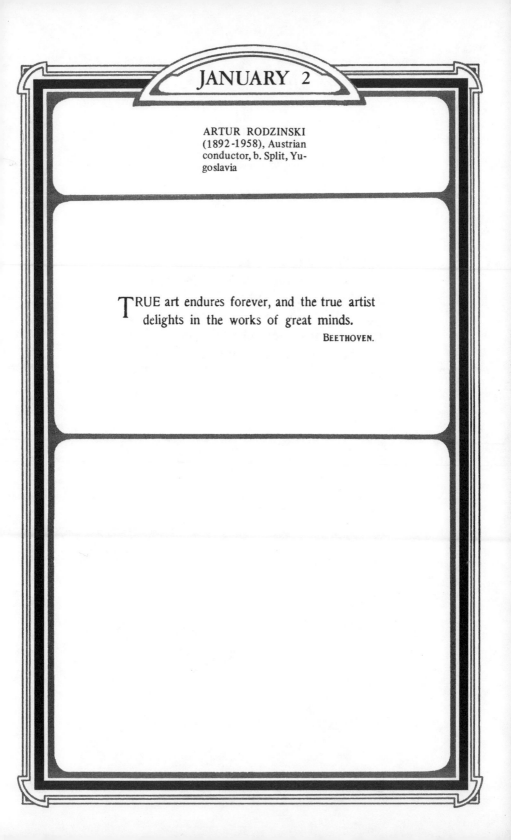

ARTUR RODZINSKI
(1892-1958), Austrian
conductor, b. Split, Yu-
goslavia

TRUE art endures forever, and the true artist
delights in the works of great minds.

BEETHOVEN.

JANUARY 3

PIETRO METASTASIO
(1698-1782), poet and
renowned opera librettist
(Handel, Gluck, Mozart
et al.), b. Rome

MUSIC is at once the product of feeling
and knowledge, for it requires from its
disciples, composers and performers alike, not
only talent and enthusiasm, but also that
knowledge and perception which are the result
of protracted study and reflection.

BERLIOZ.

GIOVANNI BATTISTA PERGOLESI
(1710-1736), Italian composer, b, Jesi,
near Ancona

BEETHOVEN! how much lies in that word! In the deep tones of the syllables there seems to sound a presentiment of immortality. I even think no other written characters but these would suit his name. SCHUMANN.

ARTURO BENEDETTI MICHELANGELI,
Italian pianist, b. Brescia (1920)

WHAT love is to man, music is to the arts and to mankind. Music is love itself, — it is the purest, most ethereal language of passion, showing in a thousand ways all possible changes of color and feeling; and though true in only a single instance, it yet can be understood by thousands of men — who all feel differently. C. M. VON WEBER.

JANUARY 6

ALEXANDER SCRIABIN
(1872 - 1915), innovative
Russian composer (Poem of
Ecstasy), b. Moscow

M USIC has, like society, its laws of propriety and etiquette; and even those to
whom their deeper meaning has not been revealed, are bound to respect and conform to
them.   LISZT.

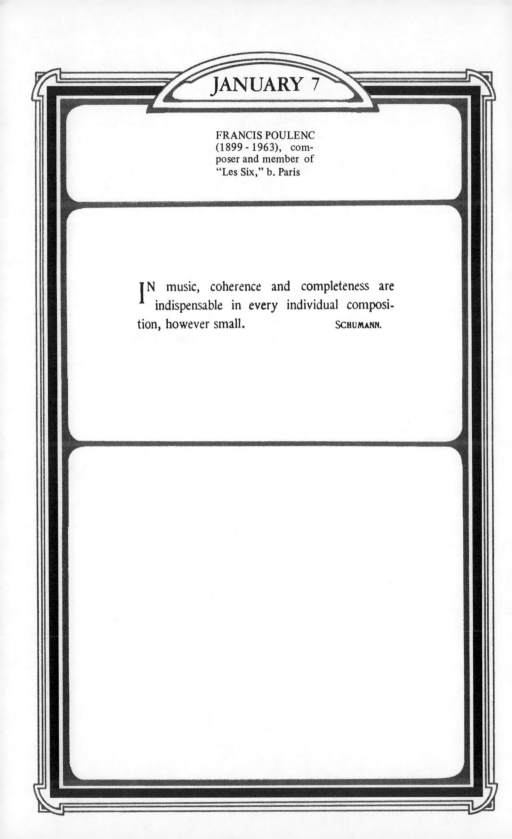

FRANCIS POULENC
(1899 - 1963), com-
poser and member of
"Les Six," b. Paris

IN music, coherence and completeness are
indispensable in every individual composition, however small.   SCHUMANN.

JANUARY 8

ELVIS PRESLEY
(1935-1977) U.S.
singer, b, Tupelo,
Miss.

Bᴿᴼᴬᴰ paths are open to every endeavor, and a sympathetic recognition is assured to every one who consecrates his art to the divine services of a conviction of a consciousness. Lɪꜱᴢᴛ.

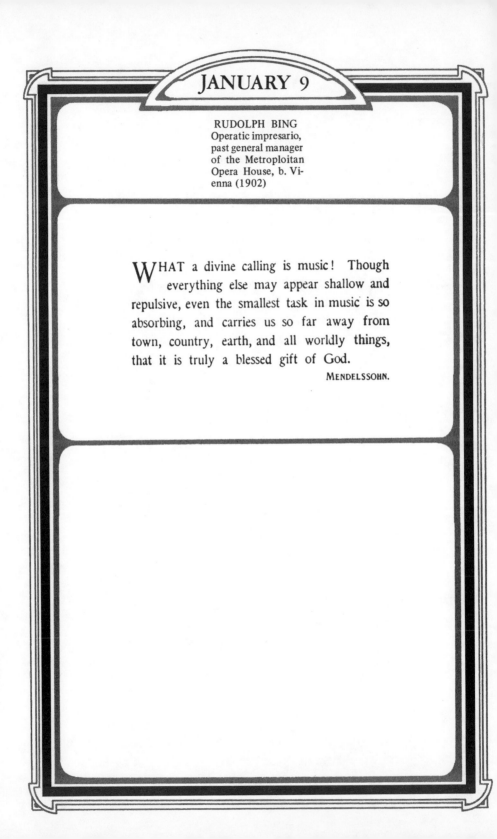

JANUARY 9

RUDOLPH BING
Operatic impresario,
past general manager
of the Metroploitan
Opera House, b. Vi-
enna (1902)

WHAT a divine calling is music! Though everything else may appear shallow and repulsive, even the smallest task in music is so absorbing, and carries us so far away from town, country, earth, and all worldly things, that it is truly a blessed gift of God.

MENDELSSOHN.

JOHANN RUDOLF ZUMSTEEG
(1770 - 1802), German opera and
song composer, b. Oldenwald

I THINK sometimes, could I only have music
on my own terms, could I live in a great
city, and know where I could go whenever I
wished the ablution and inundation of musical
waves, that were a bath and a medicine.

EMERSON.

REINHOLD GLIÈRE
(1875-1956), Russian
composer, b. Kiev

M USIC may be termed the universal language of mankind, by which human
feelings are made equally intelligible to all.

LISZT.

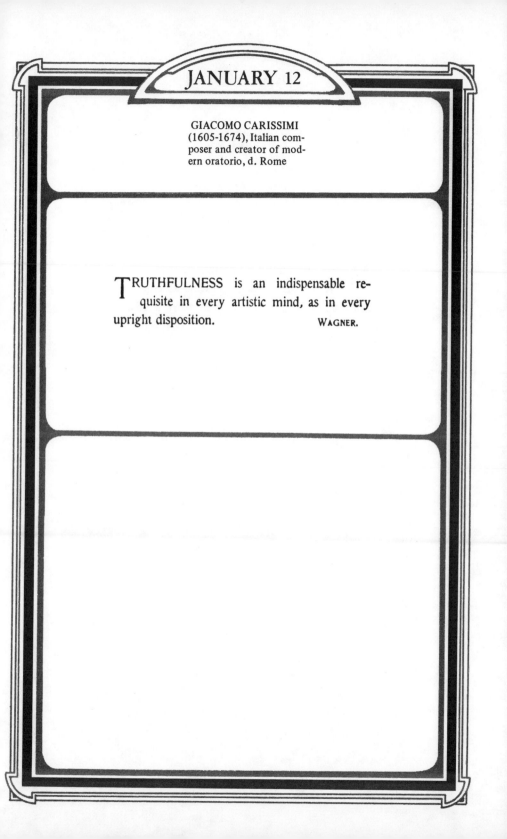

GIACOMO CARISSIMI
(1605-1674), Italian com-
poser and creator of mod-
ern oratorio, d. Rome

T RUTHFULNESS is an indispensable requisite in every artistic mind, as in every
upright disposition.   WAGNER.

STEPHEN FOSTER
(1826-1864), U.S. song
composer, d. New York
City

M USIC would have no right to exist as an
art, if that which it expresses could be
painted in oil or rendered by so many words.

FERDINAND HILLER.

JANUARY 14

ALBERT SCHWEITZER
(1875 - 1965), organist,
physician, biographer of
J. S. Bach, Nobel laureate,
b. Alsace

MUSIC is the outflow of a beautiful
mind.   SCHUMANN.

GENE KRUPA
(1909-1973, U.S.
jazz drummer, b.
Chicago

MUSIC is to the other arts, considered as a whole, what religion is to the church.

WAGNER.

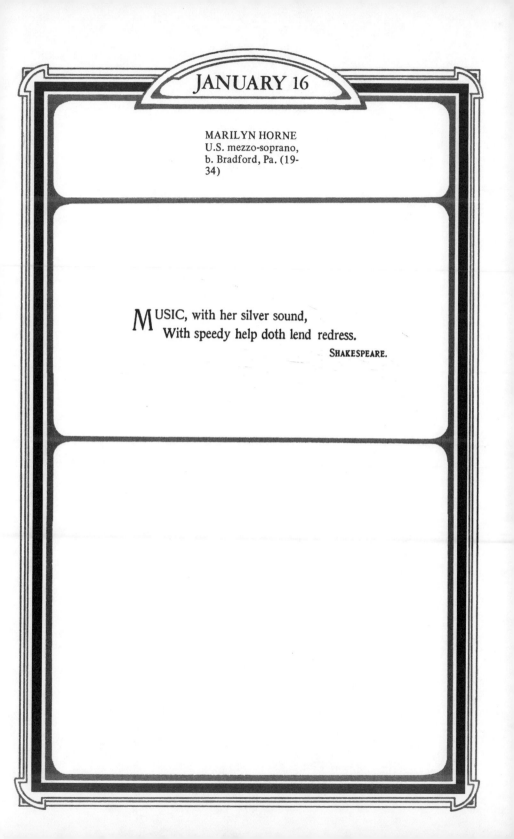

JANUARY 16

MARILYN HORNE
U.S. mezzo-soprano,
b. Bradford, Pa. (19-
34)

M USIC, with her silver sound,
With speedy help doth lend redress.

SHAKESPEARE.

JANUARY 17

FRANÇOIS JOSEPH GOSSEC
(1734-1829), Belgian symphonic and operatic composer, b.
Vergnies

WHATEVER the relations of music, it will
never cease to be the noblest and purest
of arts. . . . Its inherent solemnity makes it so
chaste and wonderful, that it ennobles whatever
comes in contact with it.   WAGNER.

EMANUEL CHABRIER
(1841-1894), French com-
poser (Espana), b. Ambert

TO me, it is with Bach as if the eternal harmonies discoursed with one another.

GOETHE.

JANUARY 19

First performance of Giuseppe
Verdi's "Il Trovatore", Rome
(1853)

MUSIC is the harmonious voice of creation,
an echo of the invisible world, one note
of the divine concord which the entire universe
is destined one day to sound.   MAZZINI.

JANUARY 20

ERNEST CHAUSSON
(1855-1899), French
composer, b. Paris

M ELODY, both vocal and instrumental, is for
the raising up of men's hearts, and the
sweetening their affections toward God.

HOOKER.

JOHN DOWLAND
(1562-1626), English lutenist
and court composer, d. London

A SONG will outlive all sermons in the memory.   H. GILES.

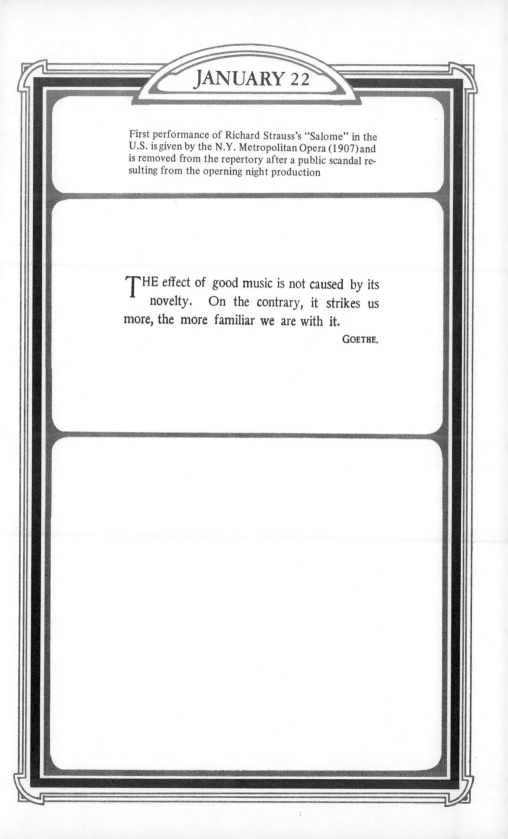

First performance of Richard Strauss's "Salome" in the U.S. is given by the N.Y. Metropolitan Opera (1907) and is removed from the repertory after a public scandal resulting from the operning night production

THE effect of good music is not caused by its novelty. On the contrary, it strikes us more, the more familiar we are with it.

GOETHE.

MUZIO CLEMENTI
(1752-1832), Italian-
English composer, pi-
anist and pedagogue,
b. Rome

M USIC is the language spoken by angels.

LONGFELLOW.

" G ENIUS is industry," says Schiller, " Genius
is patience," says Buffon, and " Genius
is an inexhaustible power of taking trouble,"
says Thomas Carlyle.

JANUARY 24

NORMAN DELLO JOIO
U.S. composer, b. New
York City (1913)

S UCH sweet compulsion doth in music lie.

MILTON.

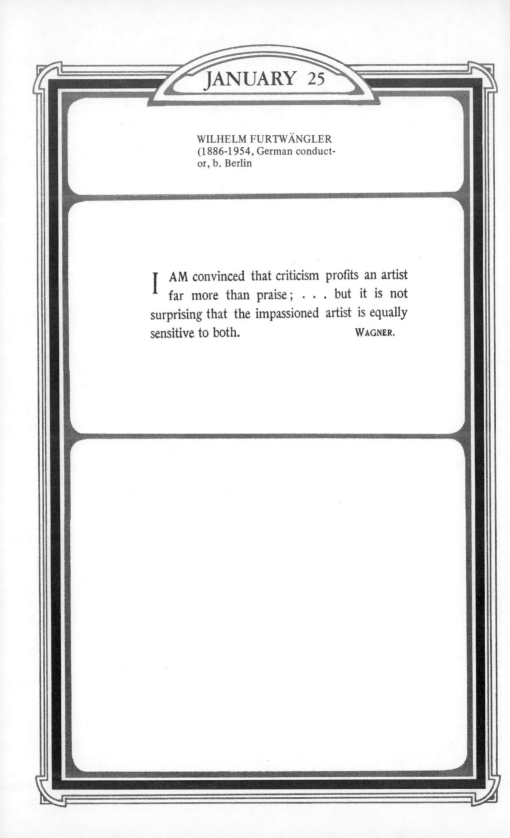

WILHELM FURTWÄNGLER
(1886-1954, German conduct-
or, b. Berlin

I AM convinced that criticism profits an artist far more than praise; . . . but it is not surprising that the impassioned artist is equally sensitive to both.   WAGNER.

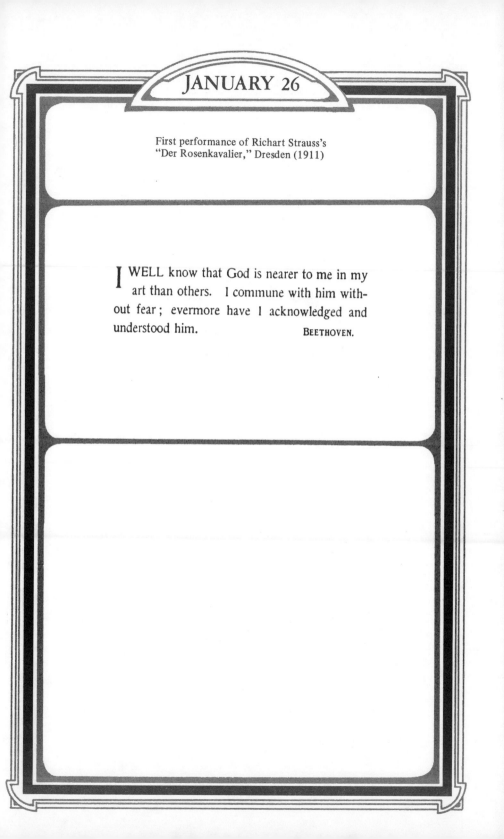

JANUARY 26

First performance of Richart Strauss's
"Der Rosenkavalier," Dresden (1911)

I WELL know that God is nearer to me in my art than others. I commune with him without fear; evermore have I acknowledged and understood him. BEETHOVEN.

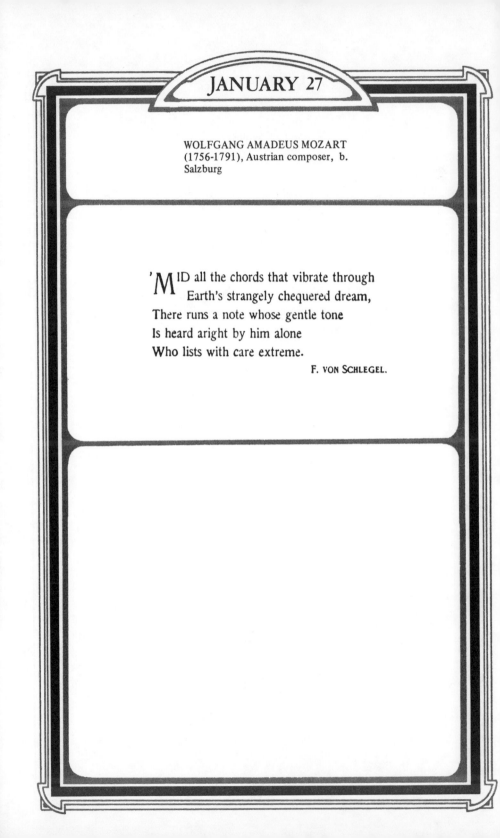

WOLFGANG AMADEUS MOZART
(1756-1791), Austrian composer, b.
Salzburg

'MID all the chords that vibrate through
    Earth's strangely chequered dream,
There runs a note whose gentle tone
Is heard aright by him alone
Who lists with care extreme.

F. VON SCHLEGEL.

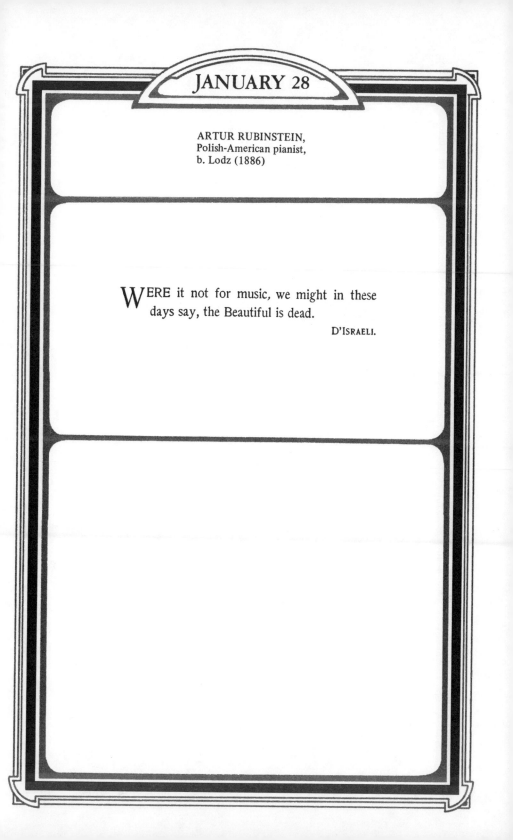

JANUARY 28

ARTUR RUBINSTEIN,
Polish-American pianist,
b. Lodz (1886)

W ERE it not for music, we might in these
days say, the Beautiful is dead.

D'ISRAELI.

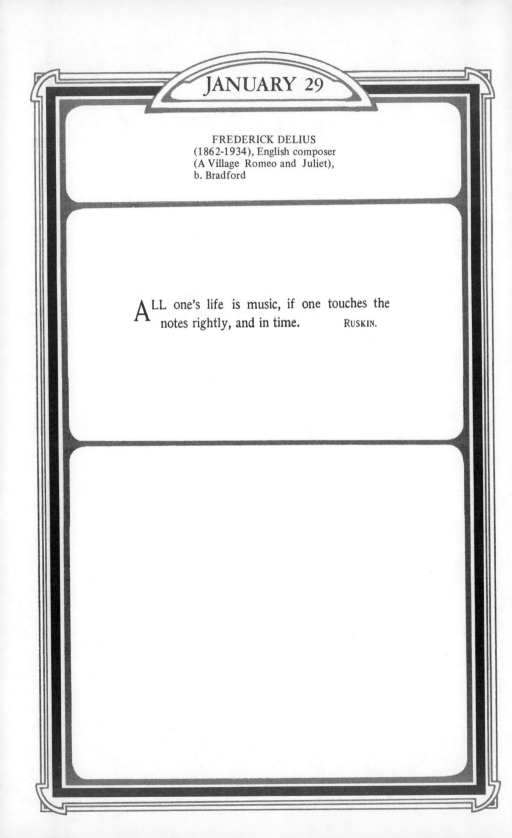

FREDERICK DELIUS
(1862-1934), English composer
(A Village Romeo and Juliet),
b. Bradford

A LL one's life is music, if one touches the
notes rightly, and in time.　　　RUSKIN.

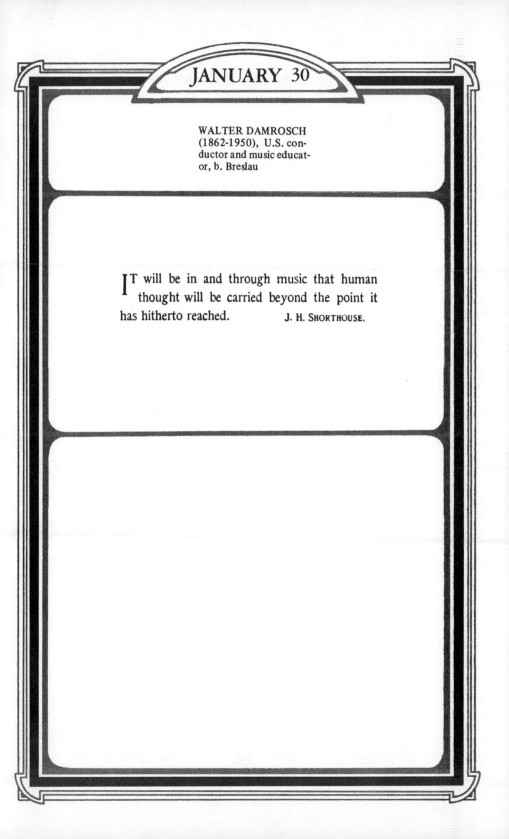

WALTER DAMROSCH
(1862-1950), U.S. con-
ductor and music educat-
or, b. Breslau

IT will be in and through music that human
thought will be carried beyond the point it
has hitherto reached.   J. H. SHORTHOUSE.

JANUARY 31

FRANZ SCHUBERT
(1797-1828), Austrian
composer, b. Vienna

FROM the bottom of my heart do I detest
that one-sidedness of the uneducated many,
who think that their own small vocation is the
best, and that every other is a humbug.

SCHUBERT.

OH! of all the songs sung,
No songs are so sweet
As the songs with refrains,
Which repeat and repeat.

HELEN HUNT JACKSON.

FEBRUARY

ASH WEDNESDAY
1979	February 28
1980	February 20
1981	March 4
1982	February 24
1983	February 16
1984	March 7
1985	February 20
1986	February 12
1987	March 4

SHROVE TUESDAY: The day before Ash Wednesday

FEBRUARY 1

VICTOR HERBERT
(1859-1924), bandmaster and
composer of operettas (Babes
in Toyland), b. Dublin, Ireland

BY music we reach those special states of consciousness which, being without form, cannot be shaped with the mosaics of the vocabulary.   OLIVER W. HOLMES.

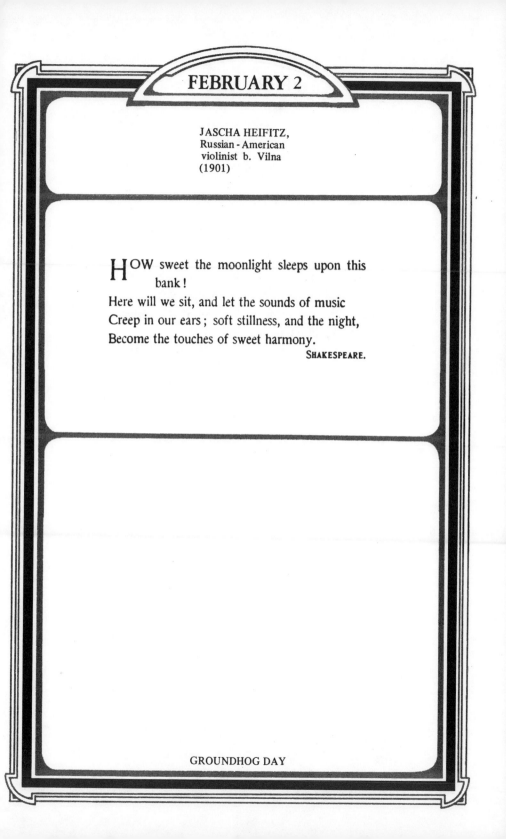

FEBRUARY 2

JASCHA HEIFITZ,
Russian - American
violinist b. Vilna
(1901)

H OW sweet the moonlight sleeps upon this
bank!
Here will we sit, and let the sounds of music
Creep in our ears; soft stillness, and the night,
Become the touches of sweet harmony.

SHAKESPEARE.

GROUNDHOG DAY

FEBRUARY 3

FELIX MENDELSSOHN
(1809-1847), German com-
poser, B. Istria

NO human art can accomplish more than
produce a rich and beautiful subject-
matter in the most perfect form, — in other
words, to blend beauty with truth.

FERDINAND HILLER.

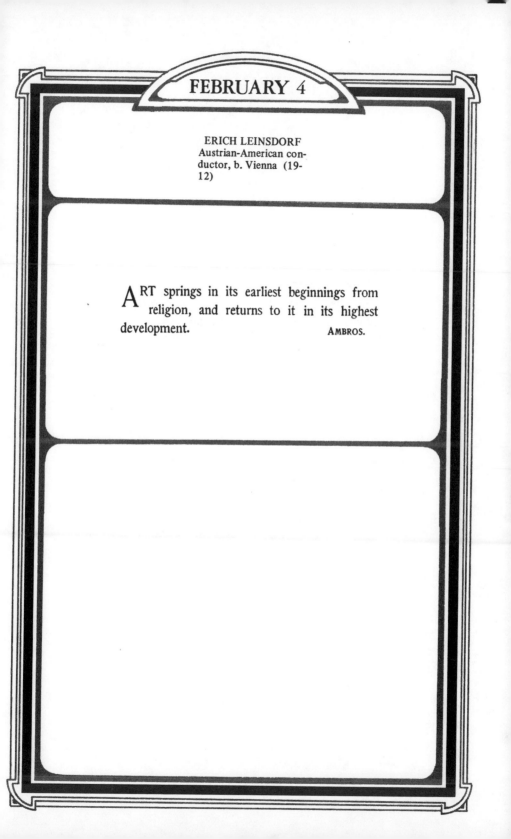

FEBRUARY 4

ERICH LEINSDORF
Austrian-American con-
ductor, b. Vienna (19-
12)

A RT springs in its earliest beginnings from
religion, and returns to it in its highest
development.   AMBROS.

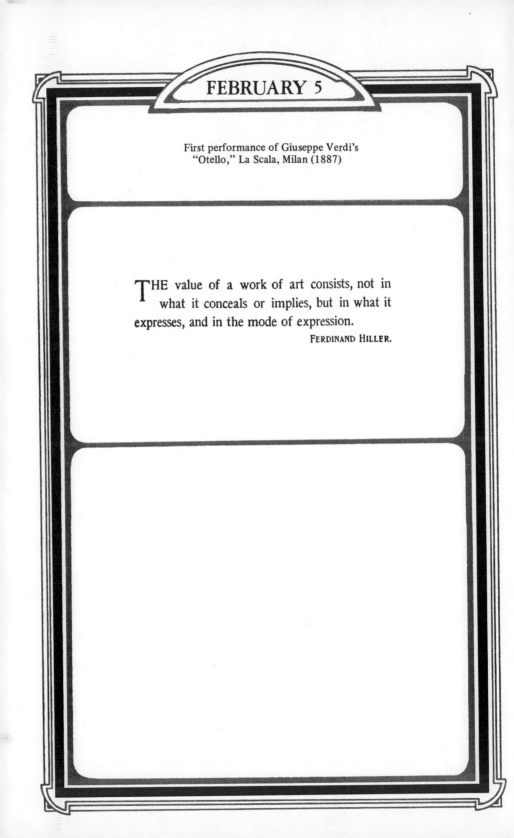

FEBRUARY 5

First performance of Giuseppe Verdi's
"Otello," La Scala, Milan (1887)

T HE value of a work of art consists, not in
what it conceals or implies, but in what it
expresses, and in the mode of expression.

FERDINAND HILLER.

FEBRUARY 6

CLAUDIO ARRAU
Chilean pianist,
b. Chilán (1903)

SOUND is the organ, but the art of sound, namely, music, is the conscious language of feeling, — of that full, overflowing love which ennobles the sensual and realizes the spiritual.

WAGNER.

FEBRUARY 7

QUINCY PORTER
(1897 - 1966), U.S.
composer and teach-
er, b. New Haven,
Conn.

MUSIC is the fourth great material want of
our natures: first food, then raiment,
then shelter, then music.   BOVEE.

FEBRUARY 8

First performance of Modest Mussorgsky's
"Boris Godunov," Maryinsky Theater, St.
Petersburg (1874)

M USIC is nothing else but wild sounds civ-
ilized into time and tune.

THOMAS FULLER.

FEBRUARY 9

ALBAN BERG
(1885-1935), Austrian composer
(Lulu, Wozzeck), b. Vienna

WITHOUT the aid of poetry, music can awaken the affections by her magic influence, producing at her will, and that instantly, serenity, complacency, pleasure, delight, ecstasy, melancholy, woe, pain, terror, and distraction.   DR. CROTCH.

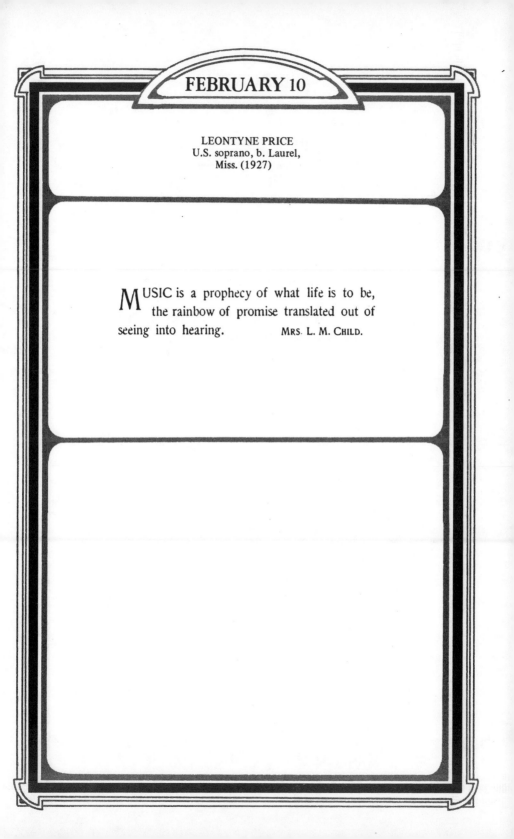

FEBRUARY 10

LEONTYNE PRICE
U.S. soprano, b. Laurel,
Miss. (1927)

M USIC is a prophecy of what life is to be,
the rainbow of promise translated out of
seeing into hearing.   MRS. L. M. CHILD.

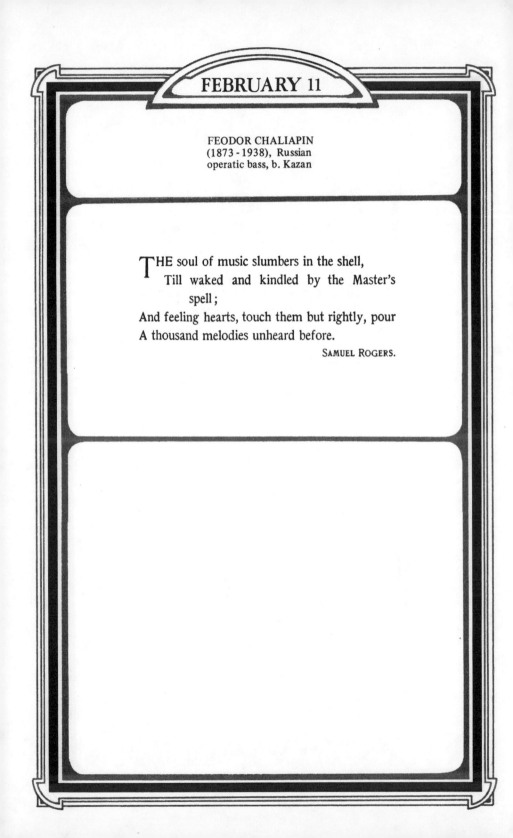

FEODOR CHALIAPIN
(1873 - 1938), Russian
operatic bass, b. Kazan

THE soul of music slumbers in the shell,
　　Till waked and kindled by the Master's
　　　spell;
And feeling hearts, touch them but rightly, pour
A thousand melodies unheard before.

SAMUEL ROGERS.

ROY HARRIS
U.S. composer, b. Lincoln
County, Nebraska (1898)

THE object of music is not to excite sensa-
tions, nor merely to imply ideas, but, by
creative power, to realize and bring ideas vividly
before our eyes.   A. B. MARX.

LINCOLN'S BIRTHDAY
(first Monday)

FEBRUARY 13

EILEEN FARRELL
U.S. soprano, b. Willi-
mantic, Conn. (1920)

NEVER judge a composition on a first hearing ; for what pleases extremely at first is
not always the best, and the works of great
masters require study.   SCHUMANN.

FEBRUARY 14

PIER FRANCESCO CAVALLI
(1602-1676), Italian opera composer (L'Ormindo), b. Crema

L IBERTY and progress are great conditions in
the empire of music, as in the universe.

BEETHOVEN.

ST. VALENTINE'S DAY

FEBRUARY 15

JEAN LANGLAIS
French organist and composer,
b. La Fontanelle (1907)

THE master-works of the past should be the
standard of the works of the present.

R. FRANZ.

FEBRUARY 16

DAVID MANNES
(1866-1959), U.S. violinist and
conductor, founder of the Mannes
College of Music (1916), b. New
York

M USIC is never stationary ; successive forms
and styles are only like so many resting-
places, — like tents pitched and taken down
again on the road to the Ideal.   LISZT.

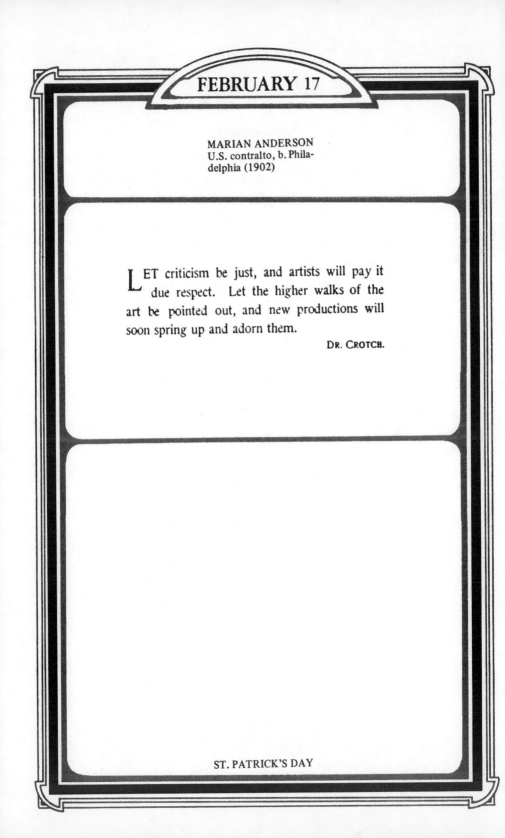

FEBRUARY 17

MARIAN ANDERSON
U.S. contralto, b. Philadelphia (1902)

L ET criticism be just, and artists will pay it due respect. Let the higher walks of the art be pointed out, and new productions will soon spring up and adorn them.

DR. CROTCH.

ST. PATRICK'S DAY

FEBRUARY 18

SIR GEORGE HENSCHEL
(1850-1934), German-British
conductor and composer, first
conductor (1881) of the Boston Symphony, b. Breslau

IT is our feelings above all that are first and
immediately affected by music.

C. M. VON WEBER.

WHERE there is no heart there can be no
music. M. HAUPTMANN.

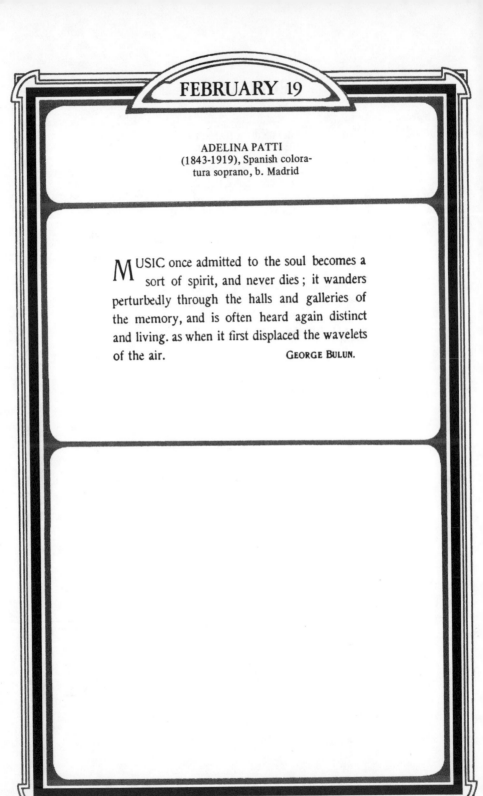

ADELINA PATTI
(1843-1919), Spanish colora-
tura soprano, b. Madrid

MUSIC once admitted to the soul becomes a sort of spirit, and never dies ; it wanders perturbedly through the halls and galleries of the memory, and is often heard again distinct and living. as when it first displaced the wavelets of the air.   GEORGE BULUN.

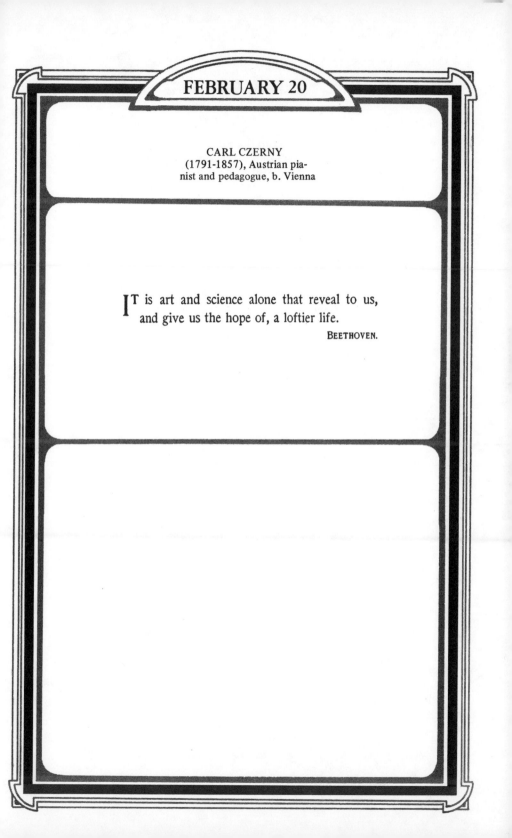

CARL CZERNY
(1791-1857), Austrian pianist and pedagogue, b. Vienna

IT is art and science alone that reveal to us,
and give us the hope of, a loftier life.

BEETHOVEN.

FEBRUARY 21

LEO DELIBES
(1836-1891), French composer of ballet
music (Coppélia), b. St.-Germain-du-Val

K EEP time.   How sour sweet music is,
When time is broke, and no proportion
kept !   SHAKESPEARE.

FEBRUARY 22

NIELS GADE
(1817-1890), Danish composer,
founder of the modern Scandi-
navian school of composition,
b. Copenhagen

SUNDAYS observe! think, when the bells do
chime,
'T is Angels' music.

GEORGE HERBERT.

WASHINGTON'S BIRTHDAY
(third Monday)

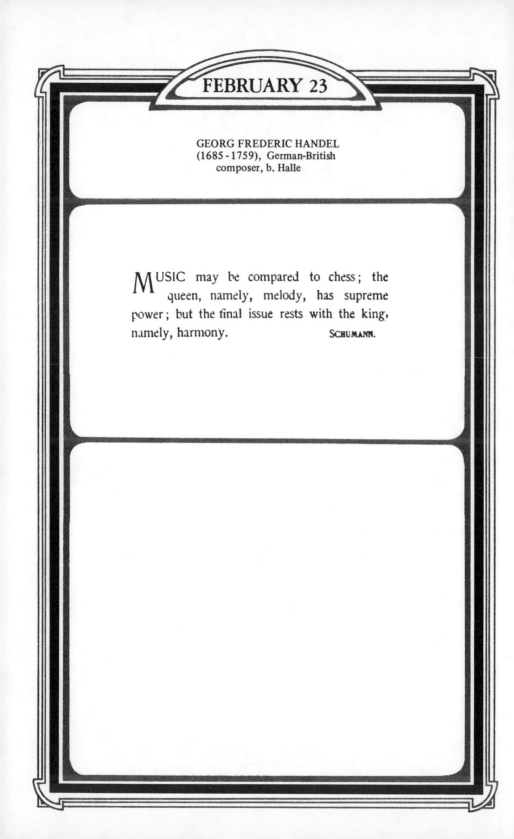

GEORG FREDERIC HANDEL
(1685 - 1759), German-British
composer, b. Halle

MUSIC may be compared to chess; the queen, namely, melody, has supreme power; but the final issue rests with the king, namely, harmony.   SCHUMANN.

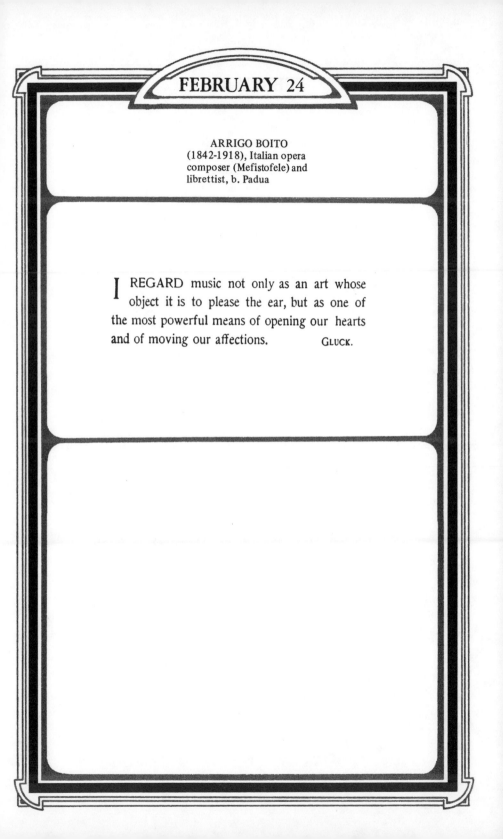

FEBRUARY 24

ARRIGO BOITO
(1842-1918), Italian opera
composer (Mefistofele) and
librettist, b. Padua

I REGARD music not only as an art whose object it is to please the ear, but as one of the most powerful means of opening our hearts and of moving our affections. GLUCK.

ENRICO CARUSO
(1873-1921), Italian
tenor, b. Naples

WHAT is the musician's calling? Is it not to send light into the deep recesses of the human heart?   SCHUMANN.

FEBRUARY 26

JOHNNY CASH
U.S. country and western
singer, b. Kingsland, Ark.
(1932)

M USIC is a more lofty revelation than all
wisdom and philosophy.

BEETHOVEN.

FEBRUARY 27

LOTTE LEHMANN
(1888-1976), German
soprano, b. Perleberg

GENIUS creates, while talent labors. Genius can dispense with artificial means, while talent is obliged to make use of them.

SCHUMANN.

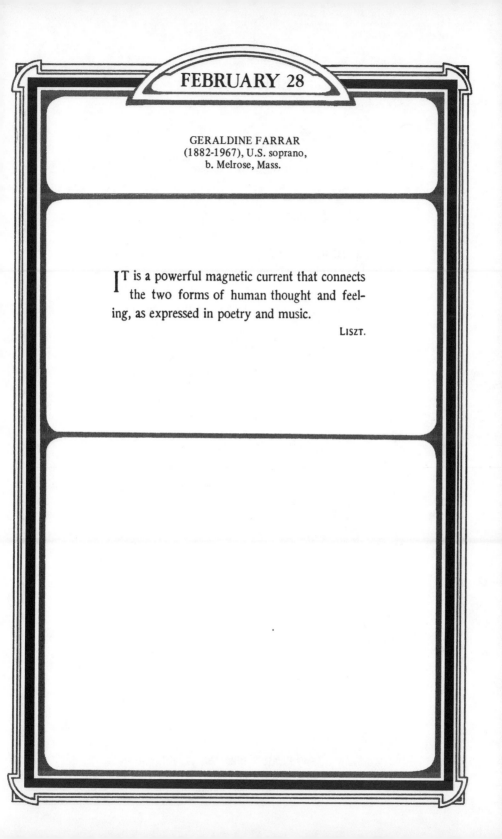

GERALDINE FARRAR
(1882-1967), U.S. soprano,
b. Melrose, Mass.

IT is a powerful magnetic current that connects the two forms of human thought and feeling, as expressed in poetry and music.

LISZT.

FEBRUARY 29

GIOACCHINO ROSSINI
(1792-1868), Italian bel canto
opera composer, b. Pesaro

WHERE music dwells
  Lingering, and wandering on as loth to
  die,
Like thoughts whose very sweetness yieldeth
  proof
That they were born for immortality.
                                    WORDSWORTH.

LEAP YEARS: 1980, 1984, 1988

MARCH

MARCH 1

GLENN MILLER
(1904-1944), trombonist and
band leader, b. Clarinda, Iowa

G OD sent His singers upon earth
With songs of sadness and of mirth,
That they might touch the hearts of men,
And bring them back to heaven again.

LONGFELLOW.

MARCH 2

KURT WEILL
(1900-1950), opera composer (The
Three-penny Opera), b. Dessau

THE man that hath no music in himself,
   Nor is not mov'd with concord of sweet
     sounds,
Is fit for treasons, stratagems, and spoils.
The motions of his spirit are dull as night,
And his affections dark as Erebus.
Let no such man be trusted.

SHAKESPEARE.

MARCH 3

First performance of Georges
Bizet's "Carmen" at the Opera
Comique, Paris (1875)

THERE is music in all things, if men had
ears.   BYRON.

MARCH 4

BERNARD HAITINK
Dutch conductor, b.
Amsterdam (1929)

M USIC washes away from the soul the dust
of every-day life.   AUERBACH.

MARCH 5

HEITOR VILLA-LOBOS
(1887-1959), Brazilian composer, b. Rio de Janerio

NEXT to theology I give to music the highest place and honor. And we see how David and all the saints have wrought their godly thoughts into verse, rhyme, and song.

MARTIN LUTHER.

MARCH 6

JULIUS RUDEL
conductor and director, N.Y.
City Opera, b. Vienna (1921)

M USIC — we love it for the buried hopes, the garnered memories, the tender feelings it can summon at a touch.

MISS L. E. LANDON.

MARCH 7

MAURICE RAVEL
(1875 - 1935), French
composer, b. Ciboure,
Basses-Pyrénées

MUSIC the fiercest grief can charm,
    And fate's severest rage disarm,
Music can soften pain to ease,
And make despair and madness please;
Our joys below it can improve,
And antedate the bliss above.   POPE.

MARCH 8

KARL PHILIPP EMANUEL BACH
(1714-1788), composer, third son
of J.S. Bach, b. Weimar

M USIC is the child of prayer, the companion of religion. CHATEAUBRIAND.

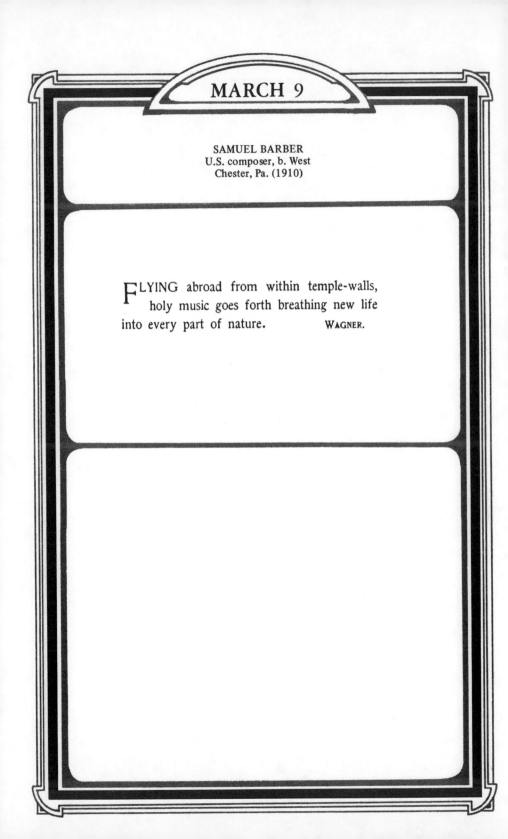

SAMUEL BARBER
U.S. composer, b. West
Chester, Pa. (1910)

FLYING abroad from within temple-walls, holy music goes forth breathing new life into every part of nature.   WAGNER.

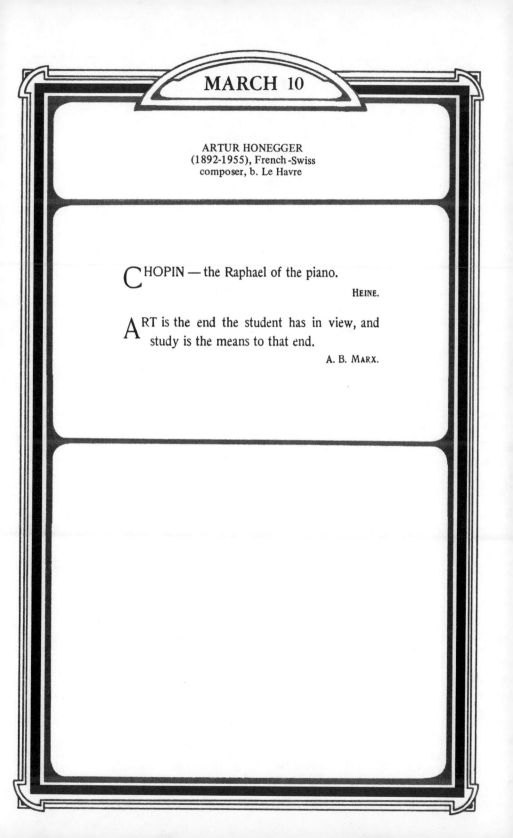

MARCH 10

ARTUR HONEGGER
(1892-1955), French-Swiss
composer, b. Le Havre

CHOPIN — the Raphael of the piano.

HEINE.

ART is the end the student has in view, and
study is the means to that end.

A. B. MARX.

CARL RUGGLES
(1876-1971), U.S. composer
(Sun-treader, Angels), b. Mar-
ion, Mass.

I KNOW of no aim more noble than that of giving music to one's native language and to one's native country.   MENDELSSOHN.

THOMAS ARNE
(1710-1770), English harpsichordist and dramatic composer (Comus), b. London

M USIC is the art of the prophets, — the only
art that can calm the agitations of the
soul; it is one of the most magnificent and
delightful presents God has given us.

MARTIN LUTHER.

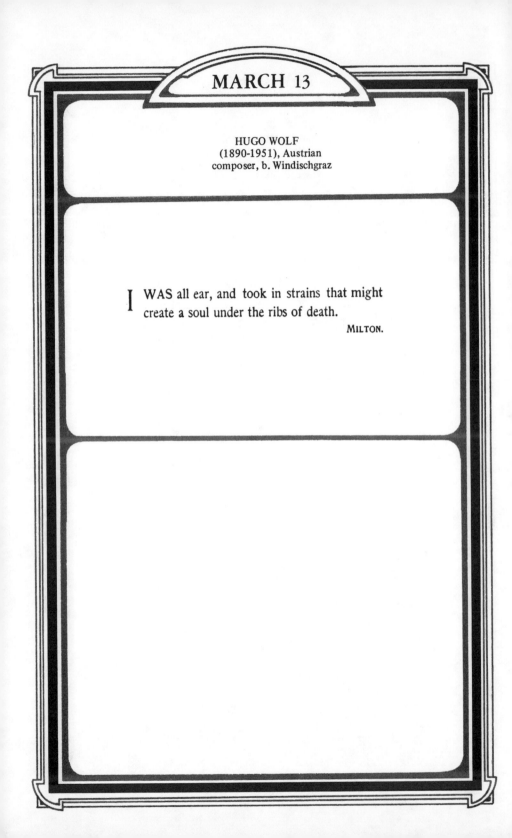

HUGO WOLF
(1890-1951), Austrian
composer, b. Windischgraz

I WAS all ear, and took in strains that might create a soul under the ribs of death.

MILTON.

JOHANN STRAUSS, SR.
(1804-1849), "Father of
the Waltz," b. Vienna

I F music be the food of love, play on.
　Give me excess of it ; that, surfeiting,
The appetite may sicken, and so die. —
That strain again ! — it had a dying fall :
O, it came o'er my ear like the sweet south,
That breathes upon a bank of violets,
Stealing and giving odor ! —　　SHAKESPEARE.

GIOVANNI RICORDI
(1785-1853), violinist and conductor, founder of the Italian
music publishing house of Ricordi, d. Milan

THE direct relation of music is not to ideas,
but emotions. Music, in the works of its
greatest masters, is more marvellous, more
mysterious, than poetry.   HENRY GILES.

CHRISTA LUDWIG
mezzo - soprano, b.
Berlin (1928)

L ORD, what music hast thou provided for
thy saints in heaven, when thou affordest
bad men such music on earth?

IZAAK WALTON.

MARCH 17

NAT "KING" COLE
(1917-1965), U.S. popular
pianist and singer, b. Mont-
gomery, Ala.

EVEN the miner, while clanking his chains, sings as he lightens his labor with untaught music; he too sings who, bending low on the oozy sand, drags the slow barge against the stream.   OVID.

MARCH 18

NIKOLAI RIMSKY-KORSAKOV
(1844-1908), Russian composer
(Scheherazade), b. Tikhvin, near
Novgorod

S WEETEST melodies are those that are by
distance made more sweet.

WORDSWORTH.

A S long as love continues the most imperious
passion, and death the surest fact of our
mingled and marvellous humanity, so long will
the sweetest and truest music on earth be ever
in the minor key. ANON.

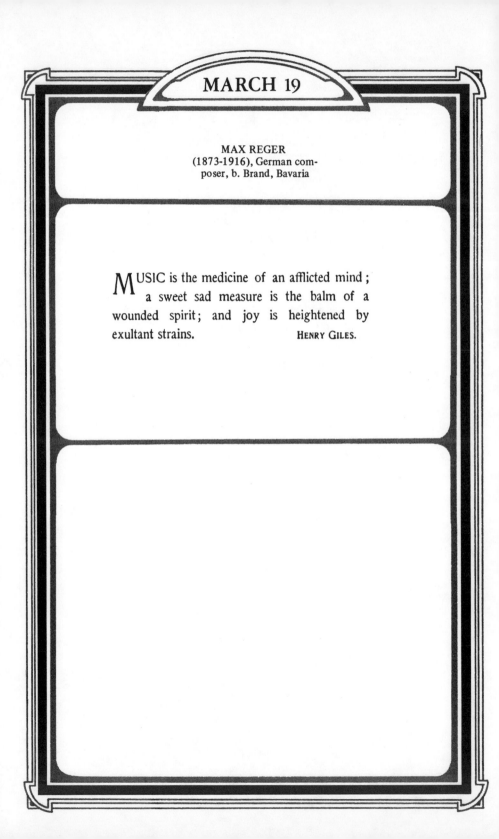

MAX REGER
(1873-1916), German com-
poser, b. Brand, Bavaria

M USIC is the medicine of an afflicted mind;
a sweet sad measure is the balm of a
wounded spirit; and joy is heightened by
exultant strains.   HENRY GILES.

LAURITZ MELCHOIR
(1890-1973), Danish tenor,
b. Copenhagen

THERE is no sweeter consolation in misfortune than the pursuit of art, for the mind employed in acquiring it sails secretly past its mishaps. ANON.

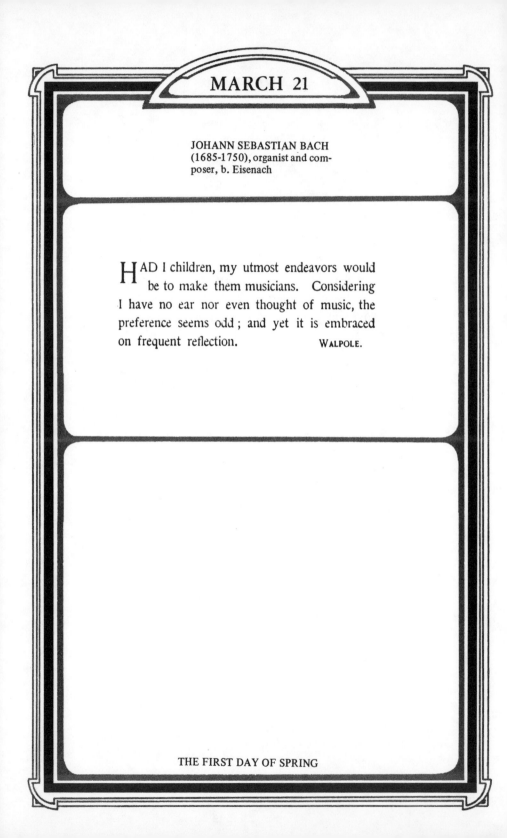

MARCH 21

JOHANN SEBASTIAN BACH
(1685-1750), organist and composer, b. Eisenach

H AD I children, my utmost endeavors would be to make them musicians. Considering I have no ear nor even thought of music, the preference seems odd ; and yet it is embraced on frequent reflection. WALPOLE.

THE FIRST DAY OF SPRING

MARCH 22

STEPHEN SONDHEIM
U.S. lyricist and composer
of stage musicals (West Side
Story, Gypsy, Company, A
Little Night Music, b. New
York City (1930)

THE science of harmony is unlimited in its scope, and we can seek the end only by going back to the beginning.

M. HAUPTMANN.

BELIEVE me, there is no greater delight than the completely uncritical frame of mind of the artist while creating.

WAGNER.

MARCH 23

EGON PETRI
(1881 - 1962), pianist and distinguished pedagogue, b. Hanover, Germany

TRUE genius, so far from imitating the productions of others which command its admiration, is only impelled to new efforts by them.   CARL MARIA VON WEBER.

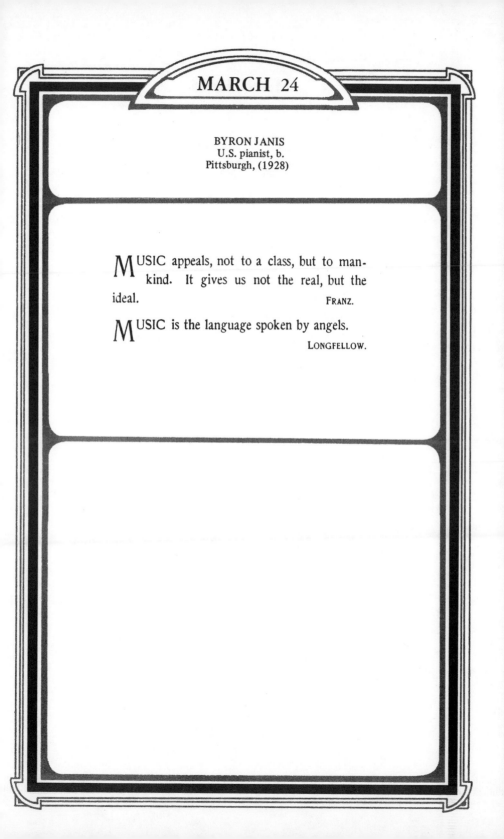

MARCH 24

BYRON JANIS
U.S. pianist, b.
Pittsburgh, (1928)

M USIC appeals, not to a class, but to mankind. It gives us not the real, but the
ideal.   FRANZ.

M USIC is the language spoken by angels.
                                    LONGFELLOW.

ARTURO TOSCANINI
(1867-1957), Italian con-
ductor, b. Parma

M USIC is indisputably the most adequate
medium of perception; and the very
essence of all perception might with truth be
termed music.   WAGNER.

MARCH 26

PIERRE BOULEZ
French conductor and
conductor, b. Mont-
brison (1925)

IT would indeed be wonderful if music were
found where there is no taste for it.

MENDELSSOHN.

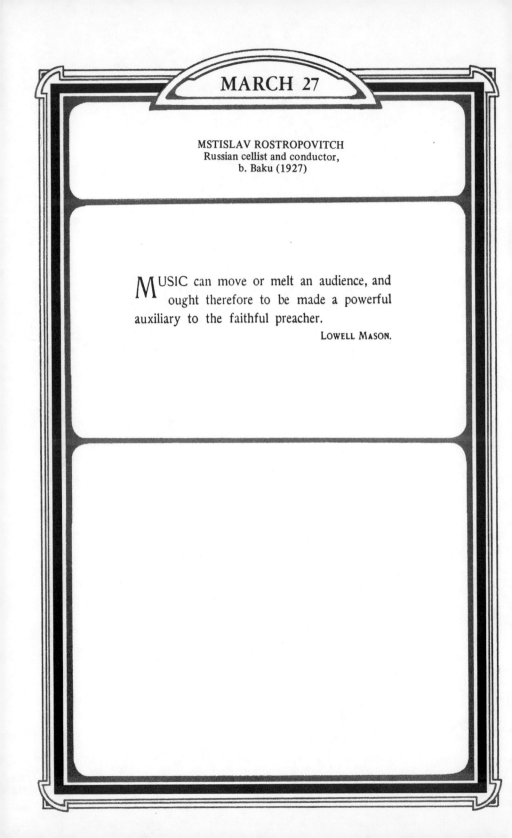

MARCH 27

MSTISLAV ROSTROPOVITCH
Russian cellist and conductor,
b. Baku (1927)

MUSIC can move or melt an audience, and ought therefore to be made a powerful auxiliary to the faithful preacher.

LOWELL MASON.

MARCH 28

RUDOLF SERKIN
pianist, b. Eger, Bo-
hemia (1903)

M USIC is the vapor of art. It is to poetry
what revery is to thought, what fluid is
to liquid, what the ocean of clouds is to the
ocean of waves.   VICTOR HUGO.

E. POWER BIGGS
(1906-1977), U.S.
organist, b. Essex,
England

GENIUS does nothing without a reason. Every artist of genius breathes into his work an unexpressed idea, which speaks to our feelings even before it can be defined.

LISZT.

CARL FRIEDRICH PETERS
(1779-1827), German music
publisher and founder of the
firm of C.F. Peters, b. Leipzig

A RT is not hereditary ; the laurels have to be
won, and a thousand hands pluck at the
wreath before it is firmly set on the artist's
head.   SCHUMANN.

FRANZ JOSEPH HAYDN
(1732-1809), Austrian composer, b. Rohrau

M USIC influences the taste and morals of a
nation no less powerfully than drama.

WAGNER.

APRIL

FIRST DAY OF PASSOVER

1979	April 12
1980	April 1
1981	April 19
1982	April 8
1983	March 29
1984	April 17
1985	April 6
1986	April 24
1987	April 14

EASTER

1979	April 15
1980	April 6
1981	April 19
1982	April 11
1983	April 3
1984	April 22
1985	April 7
1986	March 30
1987	April 19

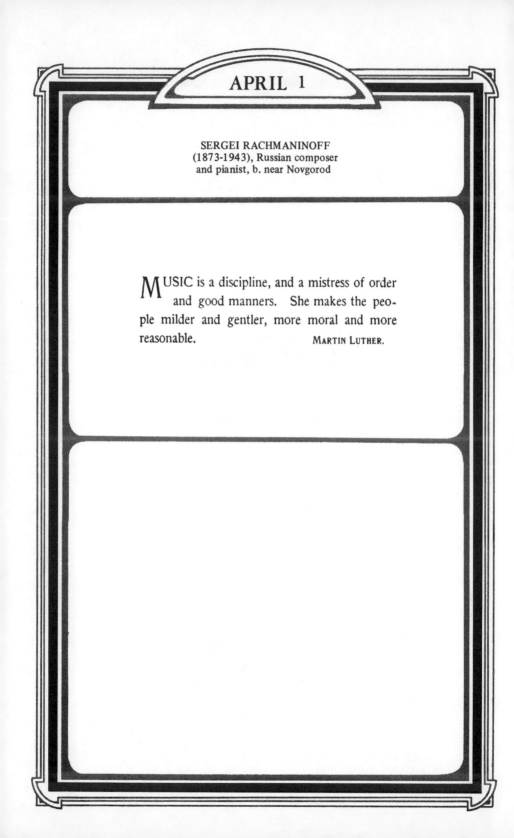

APRIL 1

SERGEI RACHMANINOFF
(1873-1943), Russian composer
and pianist, b. near Novgorod

M USIC is a discipline, and a mistress of order and good manners. She makes the people milder and gentler, more moral and more reasonable.   MARTIN LUTHER.

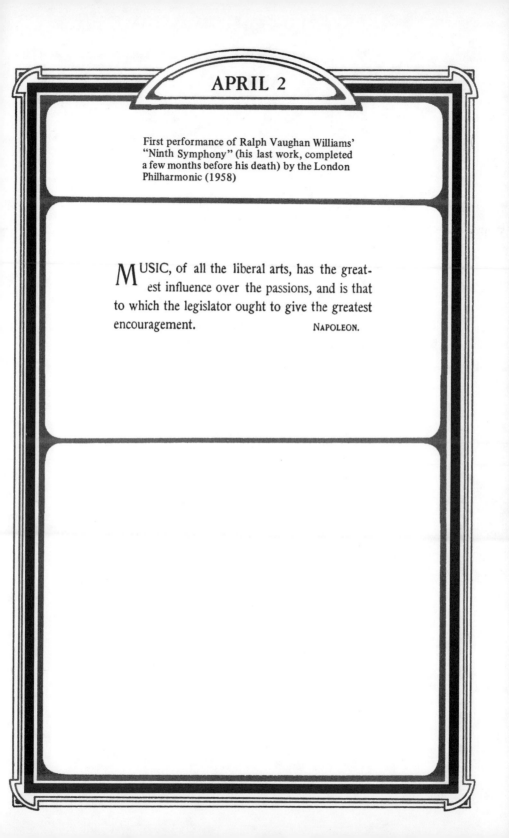

APRIL 2

First performance of Ralph Vaughan Williams'
"Ninth Symphony" (his last work, completed
a few months before his death) by the London
Philharmonic (1958)

M USIC, of all the liberal arts, has the greatest influence over the passions, and is that
to which the legislator ought to give the greatest
encouragement.   NAPOLEON.

APRIL 3

SIXTEN EHRLING
Swedish conductor,
b. Malmo (1918)

WITHOUT the definiteness of sculpture and painting, music is for that very reason far more suggestive. Like Milton's Eve, an outline, an impulse is furnished, and the imagination does the rest.　　TUCKERMAN.

PIERRE MONTEUX
(1875-1964)French-
American conductor,
b. Paris

IT is in learning music that many youthful
hearts learn love.   RICARD.

APRIL 5

HERBERT VON KARAJAN
Austrian conductor, b. Salzburg (1908)

AMONG the instrumentalities of love and peace, surely there can be no sweeter, softer, more effective voice than that of gentle, peace-breathing music. ELIHU BURRITT.

ANDRÉ PREVIN
U.S. conductor, composer,
pianist, b. Berlin (1929)

MUSIC is the only sensual gratification which mankind may indulge in to excess without injury to their moral or religious feelings.

ADDISON.

BILLIE HOLIDAY
(1915-1959), U.S. jazz
singer, b. Baltimore

SUCH is the sociableness of music, it con-
forms itself to all companies both in mirth
and mourning; complying to improve that
passion with which it finds the auditors most
affected.   FULLER.

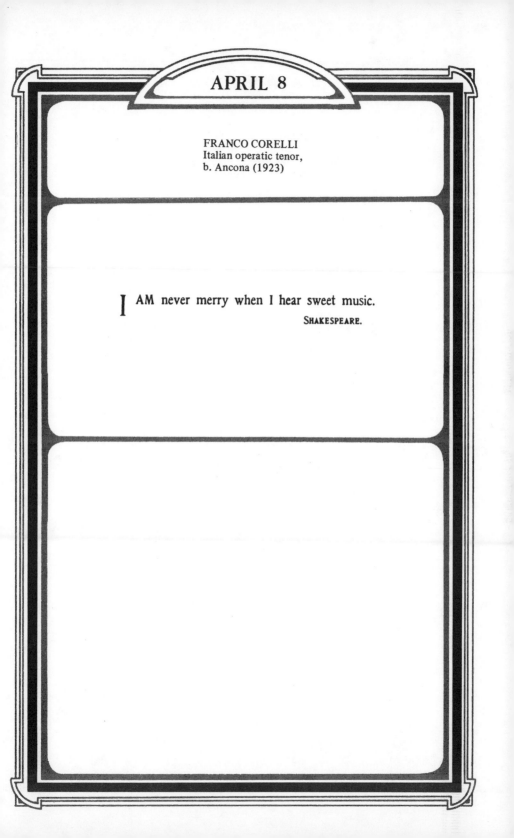

APRIL 8

FRANCO CORELLI
Italian operatic tenor,
b. Ancona (1923)

I AM never merry when I hear sweet music.

SHAKESPEARE.

PAUL ROBESON
(1898-1976), U.S. actor and
bass singer, b. Princeton, N.J.

M USIC is well said to be the speech of
angels.   CARLYLE.

M USIC is the medicine of the breaking
heart.   A. HUNT.

First performance of Johannes
Brahms's "Ein Deutsches Requiem," Bremen Cathedral, (1868)

M USIC would, indeed, be a miserable art if
it were able to describe affections only by
sounds, without language and symbols !

SCHUMANN.

APRIL 11

ALBERTO GINASTERA
Argentine composer (Bomarzo,
Beatrix Cenci), b. Buenos Aires
(1916)

M USIC is one of the fairest and most glorious gifts of God, to which Satan is a
bitter enemy; for it removes from the heart
the weight of sorrow and the fascination of evil
thoughts.   MARTIN LUTHER.

LILY PONS
French American colortura
soprano, b. Draguignon (1904)

THERE are many things in music which must be imagined without being heard. It is the intelligent hearers who are endowed with that imagination whom we should endeavor to please more particularly.   C. PH. E. BACH.

APRIL 13

First performance of George
Frederic Handel's "Messiah"
given at the New Musick Hall,
Dublin (1742)

MUSIC, the daughter rather than the imitator
of nature, impelling us to pious thought
by its solemn, mysterious accents, appeals
directly to our feelings, and is mistress of our
deepest emotions.   C. M. VON WEBER.

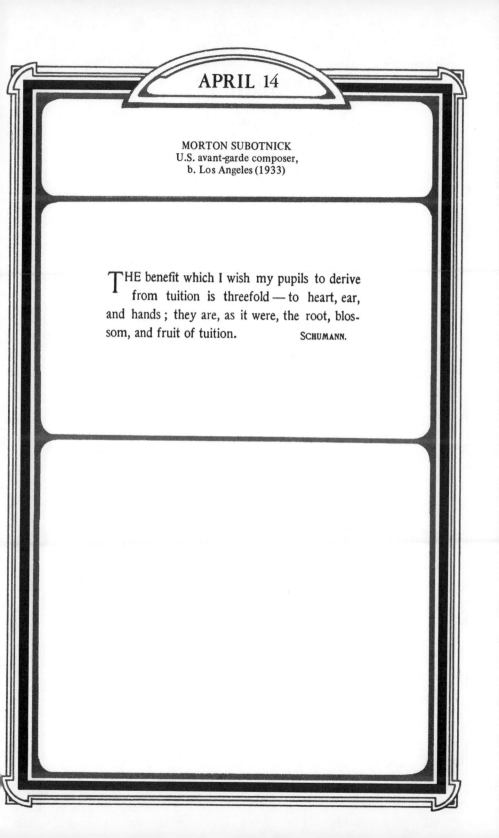

MORTON SUBOTNICK
U.S. avant-garde composer,
b. Los Angeles (1933)

THE benefit which I wish my pupils to derive from tuition is threefold — to heart, ear, and hands ; they are, as it were, the root, blossom, and fruit of tuition.   SCHUMANN.

APRIL 15

First performance of Manuel de
Falla's ballet "El Amore Brujo,"
Madrid (1915)

TRUE science and true art and true law all
spring from the great source, God. Ought
we to disregard them? Should we choose to?
Rather, in recognizing and observing them, may
we not find ourselves approaching slowly but
steadily towards Him who alone is perfect and
who alone can render us so?

STEPHEN A. EMERY.

APRIL 16

HENRY MANCINI
U.S. film and popular
composer, b. Cleveland
(1924)

IT is the artist's lofty mission to shed light on
the human soul.   SCHUMANN.

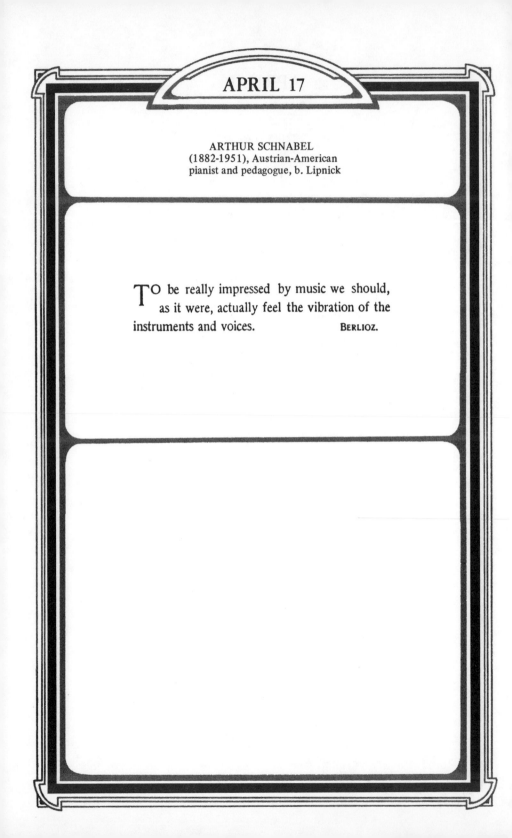

ARTHUR SCHNABEL
(1882-1951), Austrian-American
pianist and pedagogue, b. Lipnick

TO be really impressed by music we should, as it were, actually feel the vibration of the instruments and voices.   BERLIOZ.

LEOPOLD STOKOWSKI
(1882-1977), American conductor, b. London

M USIC, as a branch of education, should not
be wanting in any nation in which there
is a natural taste for it.   A. B. MARX.

APRIL 19

First performance of Christoph
Willibald Gluck's opera, "Iphigé-
nie en Aulide," Paris (1774)

THERE is a certain profound beauty in music which, though we can all feel and perceive it, is yet by no means of a kind to call forth applause.   BERLIOZ.

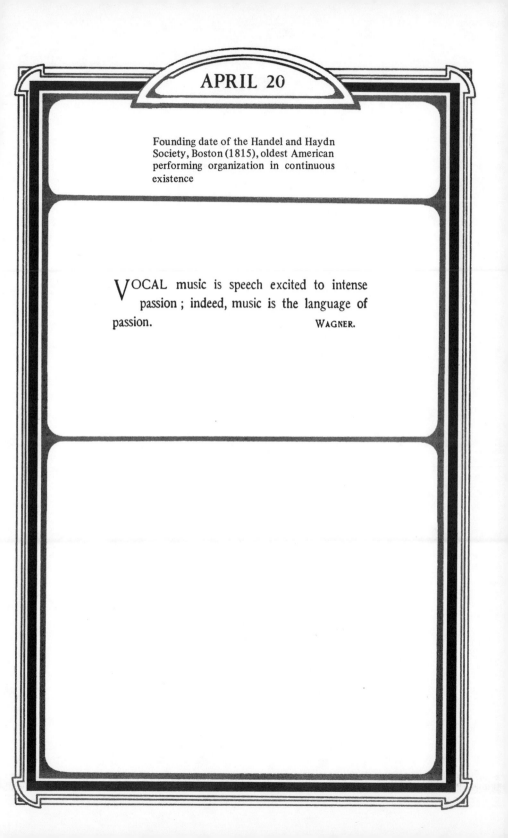

APRIL 20

Founding date of the Handel and Haydn
Society, Boston (1815), oldest American
performing organization in continuous
existence

VOCAL music is speech excited to intense
passion ; indeed, music is the language of
passion.   WAGNER.

RANDALL THOMPSON
U.S. choral composer, b.
New York City (1899)

IT is the nature of instrumental music in its highest form to express in sounds what is inexpressible in words. WAGNER.

APRIL 22

YEHUDI MENUHIN
U.S. violinist, b. New
York City, 1916

IT is owing to the very nature of music, which is pervaded by the all-reconciling element of love, that even the strongest antagonism in religious, political, philosophical views vanishes before it. FERDINAND HILLER.

APRIL 23

SERGEI PROKOFIEV
(1891-1953), Soviet com-
poser, b. Sontzovka

E XPERIENCE teaches us that the Muse
abhors and does not abide in places where
the Evil One reigns, for the wicked are not
worthy of her.   PRAETORIUS.

APRIL 24

PADRE GIAMBATTISTA MARTINI
(1706-1784), Franciscan priest, composer, and eminent teacher (of Mozart,
Gluck and others), b. Bologna

M USIC is not, indeed, like painting, an im-
itative art, but applies itself, like architecture and poetry, directly to the imagination,
without the intervention of any kind of imi-
tation.   HARRIS.

R HYTHM constitutes, as it were, the life and
soul of all music.   H. SCHÜTZ.

APRIL 25

ELLA FITZGERALD
U.S. jazz singer, b. New-
port News, Va. (1918)

WERE Music to be expelled from the House of God, it would be deprived of its highest aim and dignity . . . and like every art, when separated from religion — which is the soil on which its first germs were scattered and nursed — Music also would be ruined.

AMBROS.

APRIL 26

First performance of Charles Ives's "Fourth Symphony,"
his largest work, by the American Symphony Orchestra,
Leopold Stokowski directing, Carnegie Hall, N.Y. (1965)

M USIC should kindle the divine flame in the
human mind.   BEETHOVEN.

APRIL 27

NICOLAS SLONIMSKY
Russian-American conductor and
music lexicographer, b. St. Petersburg (1894)

IF your music emanates from your very heart,
it will have a reciprocal effect on others.

SCHUMANN.

JOHN JACOB NILES
U.S. folksinger and suthority
on folk music, b. Louisville,
Ky. (1892)

MUSIC moves us, and we know not why; we feel the tears, and cannot trace the source. Is it the language of some other state, born of its memory? For what can wake the soul's strong instinct of another world, like music?   LETITIA E. LANDON.

EDWARD KENNEDY ("DUKE") ELLINGTON
(1899-1974), U.S. jazz pianist and composer, b.
Washington, D.C.

INSPIRATION is, after all, the noblest attri-
bute in an artist.   MORITZ HAUPTMANN.

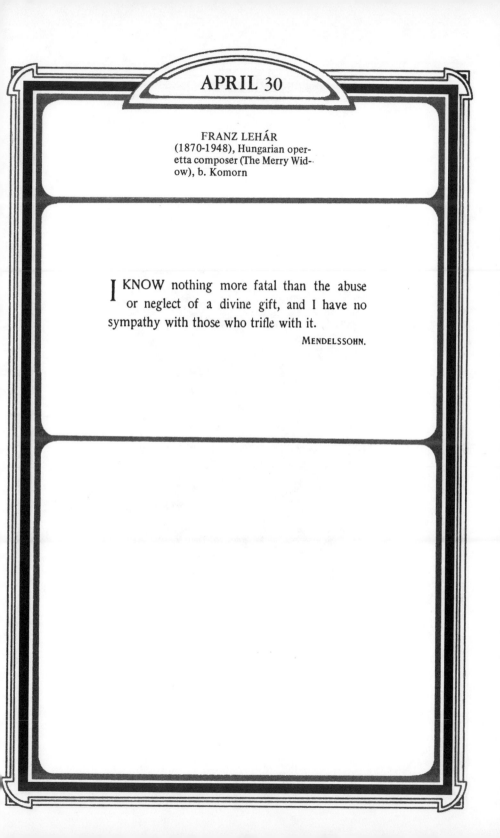

APRIL 30

FRANZ LEHÁR
(1870-1948), Hungarian operetta composer (The Merry Widow), b. Komorn

I KNOW nothing more fatal than the abuse
or neglect of a divine gift, and I have no
sympathy with those who trifle with it.

MENDELSSOHN.

MOZART'S BIRTHPLACE IN SALZBURG

MAY

ASCENSION DAY: Ten days before Pentecost

MOTHER'S DAY: The second Sunday

MEMORIAL DAY: The last Monday

MAY 1

LEO SOWERBY
U.S. composer, b. Grand
Rapids, Mich. (1895)

THAT musician especially who is inspired by
nature, without copying her, breathes out
in tones the tenderest secrets of his destiny ; he
thinks, feels, and speaks through her.

LISZT.

ALESSANDRO SCARLATTI
(1660-1725), opera composer, founder of
the Neopolitan school of opera composition,
b. Palmero

M USIC is a heavenly art ; nothing supplants
it except true love.   BERLIOZ.

MAY 3

BING CROSBY
(1903-1977), U.S. popular
singer, b. Tacoma, Wash.

MENDELSSOHN is a man to whom I look up as to some lofty mountain. He is a true divinity, and no day passes in which he does not utter at least two ideas worthy to be graven on gold.   SCHUMANN.

MAY 4

ROBERTA PETERS
U.S. operatic soprano,
b. New York City (1930)

NO one has ever felt more devoutly than
Bach, more happily than Mozart, or with
more gigantic power than Beethoven.

KULLAK.

MAY 5

HANS PFITZNER
(1869-1949), German
composer, b. Moscow,
Russia

IT is idle to talk of the defects of music;
progress and reform — that's the question.

MENDELSSOHN.

MAY 6

GEORGE PERLE
U.S. composer and theorist,
b. Bayonne, N.J. (1915)

M USIC is God's best gift to man,
  The only art of Heaven given to earth,
The only art of earth we take to Heaven.

LANDON.

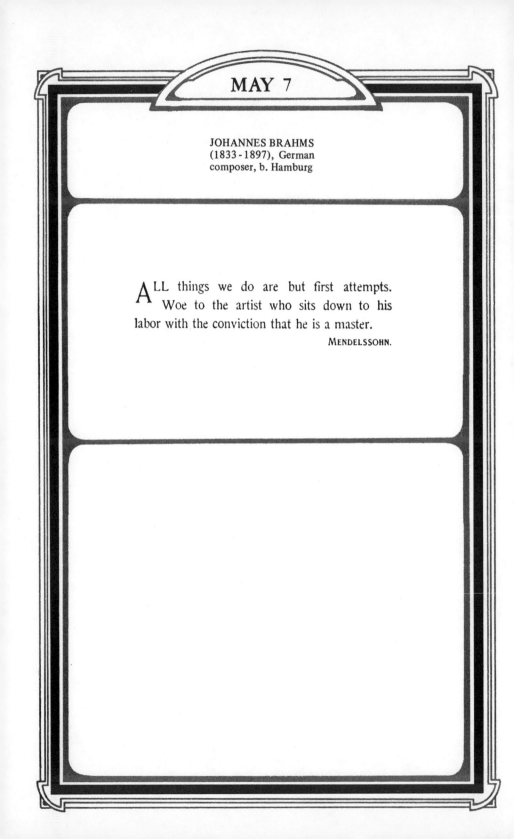

MAY 7

JOHANNES BRAHMS
(1833 - 1897), German
composer, b. Hamburg

A_{LL} things we do are but first attempts.
Woe to the artist who sits down to his
labor with the conviction that he is a master.

MENDELSSOHN.

MAY 8

LOUIS MOREAU GOTTSCHALK
(1829-1869), U.S. pianist and composer, b. New Orleans

WHAT is genius else than a priestly power revealing God to the human soul?

LISZT.

MAY 9

DIETRICH BUXTEHUDE
(c. 1637-1707), German organist and composer who strongly
influenced J.S. Bach, d. Lubeck

THE sound is in the execution of the pianist
what color is in painting.

GOTTSCHALK.

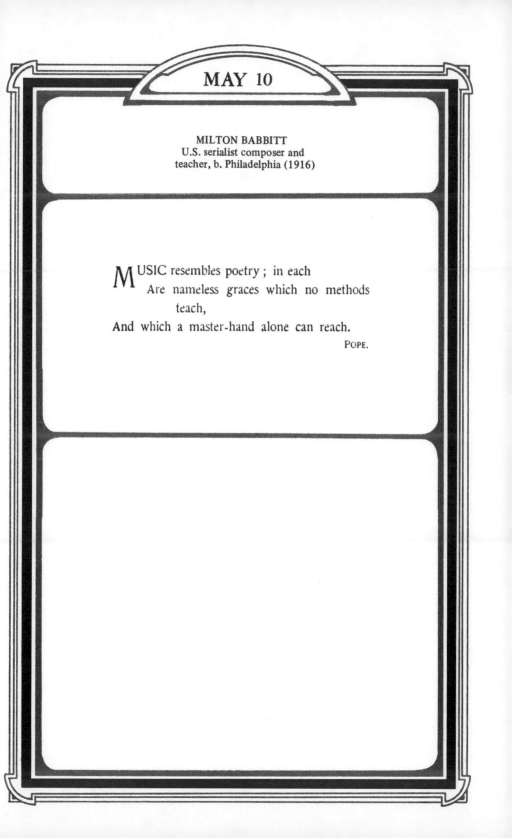

MILTON BABBITT
U.S. serialist composer and
teacher, b. Philadelphia (1916)

M USIC resembles poetry ; in each
Are nameless graces which no methods
teach,
And which a master-hand alone can reach.

POPE.

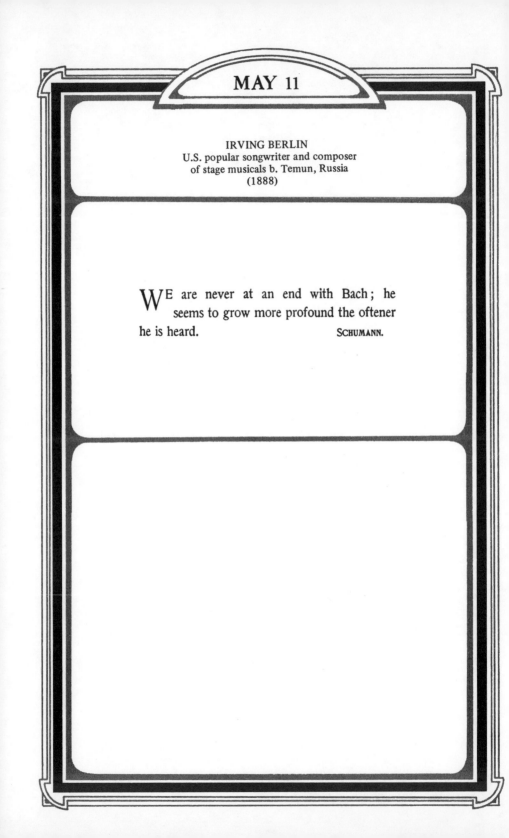

MAY 11

IRVING BERLIN
U.S. popular songwriter and composer
of stage musicals b. Temun, Russia
(1888)

WE are never at an end with Bach; he
seems to grow more profound the oftener
he is heard. SCHUMANN.

MAY 12

BURT BACHARACH
U.S. popular songwriter and
arranger, b. Kansas City, Mo.
(1928)

A RT has no fatherland, and all that is beautiful ought to be prized by us, no matter
what clime or region has produced it.

WEBER.

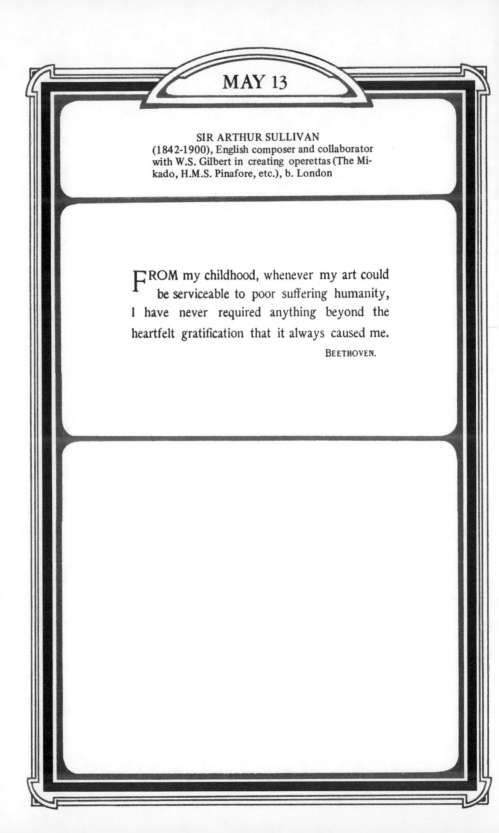

SIR ARTHUR SULLIVAN
(1842-1900), English composer and collaborator
with W.S. Gilbert in creating operettas (The Mi-
kado, H.M.S. Pinafore, etc.), b. London

FROM my childhood, whenever my art could be serviceable to poor suffering humanity, I have never required anything beyond the heartfelt gratification that it always caused me.

BEETHOVEN.

OTTO KLEMPERER
(1885-1973), German
conductor, b. Breslau

WE know they music made
    In heaven, ere man's creation ;
But when God threw it down to us that strayed,
    It dropt with lamentation,
And ever since doth its sweetness shade
    With sighs for its first station.

JEAN INGELOW.

MAY 15

CLAUDIO MONTEVERDI
(1567-1643), Italian madrigal and dramatic
composer, founder of modern opera, baptized
Cremona (day of birth unknown)

M^Y language is understood all over the
world.   HAYDN.

MAY 16

WALTER LIBERACE
U.S. popular pianist, b. West
Allis, Wisconsin (1919)

MUSIC alone has the inherent power of interpreting transcendent affections with absolute truth. In power of expression it leaves the sister-arts far behind it. FRANZ.

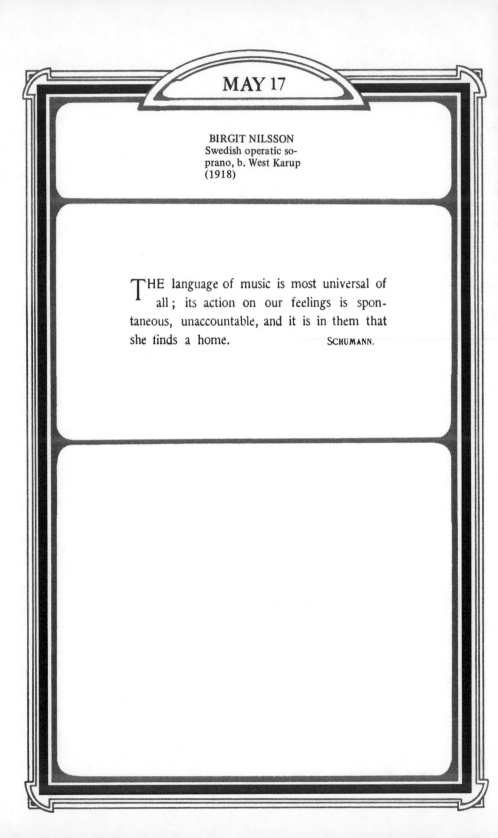

MAY 17

BIRGIT NILSSON
Swedish operatic so-
prano, b. West Karup
(1918)

THE language of music is most universal of all; its action on our feelings is spontaneous, unaccountable, and it is in them that she finds a home. SCHUMANN.

BORIS CHRISTOFF
Bulgarian bass-baritone,
b. Sofia (1918)

M USIC, as an independent art, is, properly speaking, still in its very infancy, yet grand and magnificent, the Pythian Apollo of our time.   BERLIOZ.

MAY 19

DAME MELLIE MELBA
(1861-1931), Australian
soprano, b. Melbourne

YOU will be a musician when not only your
fingers, but also your heart and mind, are
full of music.   SCHUMANN.

JERZY FITELBERG
(1903 - 1951), Polish
composer, b. Warsaw

MUSIC is the art of moving, by a systematic combination of sounds, the affections of intelligent, receptive, and cultivated beings.

BERLIOZ.

GINA BACHAUER
(1913-1976), Greek
pianist, b. Athens

THAT composer alone has penetrated the
mysteries of harmony, who by its agency
is able to act on human feelings.

E. T. A. HOFFMANN.

RICHARD WAGNER
(1813-1883), German opera
composer, b. Leipzig

M ELODY is the very life-blood of music,
and it is above all necessary that its flow
should continue and remain intact and unadulterated.   A. B. Marx.

EDMUND RUBBRA
English composer, b.
Northampton (1901)

TO engender and diffuse faith, and to pro-
mote our spiritual well-being, are among
the noblest aims of music.

C. PH. EM. BACH.

BOB DYLAN
U.S. popular singer and composer, b. Duluth, Minn. (1941)

THE one and only form of music is melody ; no music is conceivable without melody, and both are absolutely inseparable.

WAGNER.

MAY 25

BEVERLY SILLS
U.S. operatic soprano,
b. Brooklyn, N.Y. (1929)

MELODY alone constitutes the essence of all
music.   J. RAFF.

IN the midst of popular applause, how
dissatisfied an artist feels with his own
work !   GRÉTRY.

MAY 26

WILLIAM BOLCOM,
U.S. pianist and com-
poser, b. Seattle (1938)

A MUSICIAN who wishes to think correctly when composing, should have melody and harmony simultaneously in his mind.

BACH.

MARIO DEL MONACO
Italian tenor, b. Florence
(1915)

B RILLIANCY of execution is valuable only
when it serves higher purposes.

SCHUMANN.

DIETRICH FISCHER-DIESKAU
German baritone, b. Berlin (1925)

MEN of talent alone should compose music; others should work and wait until the light of perception shines upon them.

MOSCHELES.

MAY 29

First performance of Igor Stravinsky's
ballet "Le Sacre du Printemps," Théatre
des Champs-Elysées, Paris (1913)

IT is the funeral march. I did not think
That there had been such magic in sweet
sounds!   SOUTHEY.

GEORGE LONDON
American bass-baritone,
b. Montreal (1920)

A NGEL of music !   When our finest speech
    Is all too coarse to give the heart relief,
The inmost fountains lie within thy reach,
    Soother of every joy and every grief !
And to the stumbling words thou lendest wings
On which aloft th' enfranchised spirit springs.

W. ALLINGHAM.

MAY 31

First performance of Kraysztof Penderecki's
"Threnody: To the Victims of Hiroshima,"
Warsaw (1961)

THE study of thorough-bass, even though it
be superficial, conduces to the better under-
standing of good compositions, for it renders
their construction intelligible ; indeed, it is the
grammar of music, and therefore an indispensable requisite for a deeper insight into the nature
thereof.   MOSCHELES.

JUNE

FATHER'S DAY: The third Sunday

JUNE 1

IGNAZ PLEYEL
(1757-1831), Austrian pianist
and composer, b. Ruppertsthal

IT may with truth be said, that a poet's work
consists in what he leaves to imagination,
and to elucidate and express by music is the
task of the composer.   WAGNER.

JUNE 2

SIR EDWARD ELGAR
(1857-1934), English com-
poser, b. Broadheath

W HENEVER music attempts to be more
than the language of passion, it goes out
of its depth, and of necessity fails.

C. M. VON WEBER.

JUNE 3

ROLAND HAYES
(1887 - 1977), U.S.
tenor, b. Curryville,
Ga.

MEN of strong impulses alone know what love is. Love alone fathoms beauty; beauty alone creates art.   WAGNER.

JUNE 4

ROBERT MERRILL
U.S. baritone, b. Brooklyn,
N.Y. (1919)

THE main defect in music is the necessity of reproducing compositions by performing them. If it were as easy to read music as it is to read books, Beethoven's sonatas would be as popular as Schiller's poems.

FERDINAND HILLER.

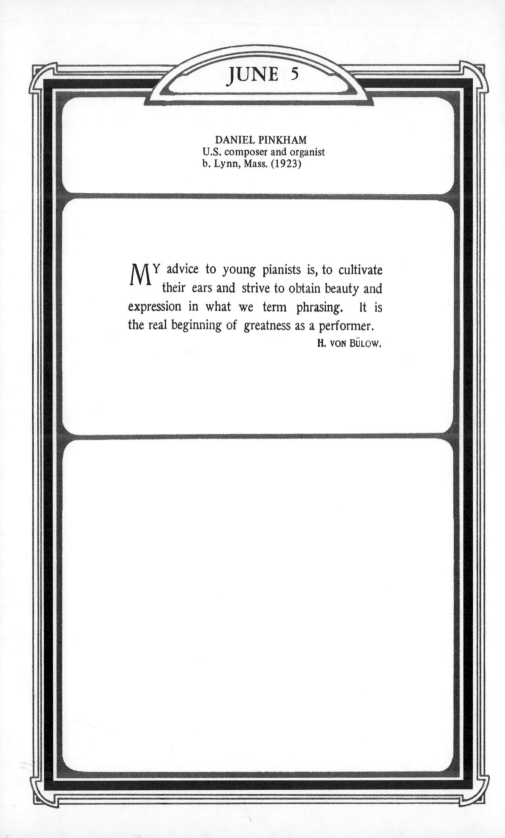

DANIEL PINKHAM
U.S. composer and organist
b. Lynn, Mass. (1923)

M Y advice to young pianists is, to cultivate
their ears and strive to obtain beauty and
expression in what we term phrasing.   It is
the real beginning of greatness as a performer.

H. VON BÜLOW.

JUNE 6

VINCENT PERSICHETTI
U.S. composer and theorist,
b. Philadelphia (1915)

ART is a bond that unites all the world.
How much closer is this bond between
true artists!   BEETHOVEN.

JUNE 7

First performance of Benjamin Britten's
opera, "Peter Grimes," Sadler's Wells
Theatre, London (1945)

A LL the arts flow from the same source ; it is
the idea embodied in a work of art, and
not the mode of enunciating it, that determines
its rank in the scale of beauty.   LISZT.

ROBERT SCHUMANN
(1810-1856), German composer
and pianist, b. Zwickau, Saxony

To invent beautiful forms of rhythm is a thing that cannot be taught. It is one of the rarest gifts in music; rhythm itself is, moreover, the least developed part of modern music.　　　　　　　　　　　　　BERLIOZ.

JUNE 9

COLE PORTER
(1892-1964), U.S. songwriter and composer
of stage musicals, b. Peru, Indiana

EVERY note of Mozart's is a round in the
ladder of the spheres, by which he ascended
to the Heaven of perfection.

JEAN PAUL RICHTER.

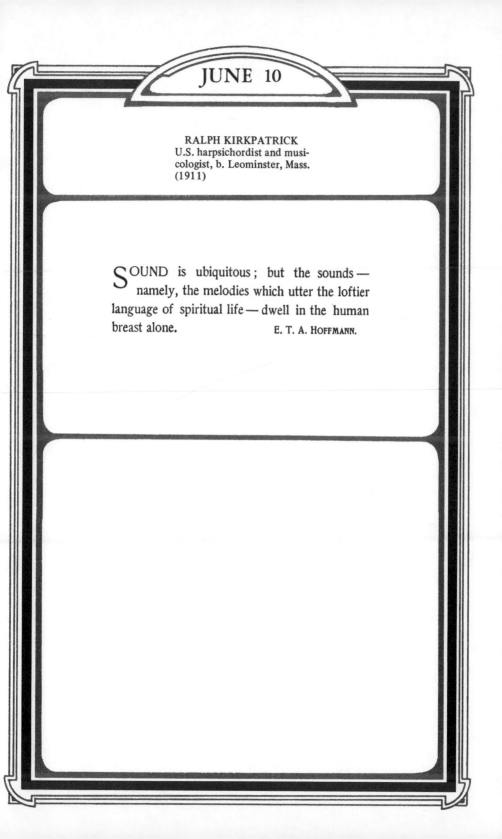

JUNE 10

RALPH KIRKPATRICK
U.S. harpsichordist and musicologist, b. Leominster, Mass.
(1911)

SOUND is ubiquitous; but the sounds — namely, the melodies which utter the loftier language of spiritual life — dwell in the human breast alone. E. T. A. HOFFMANN.

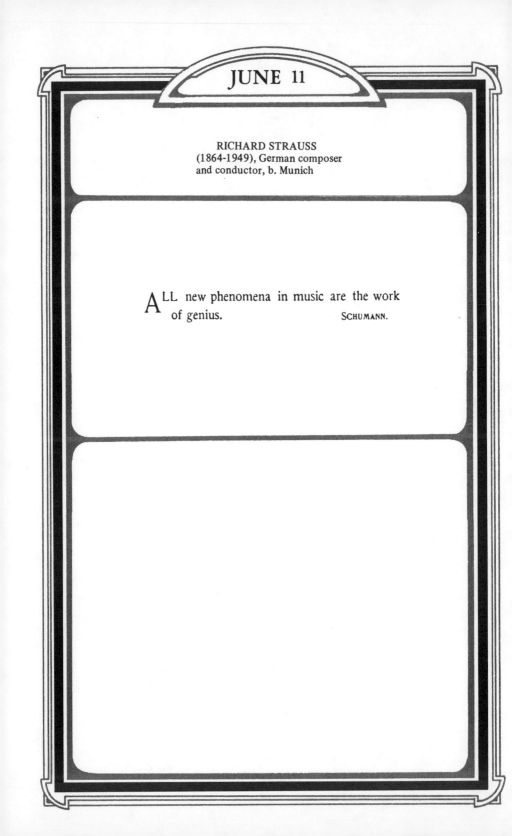

JUNE 11

RICHARD STRAUSS
(1864-1949), German composer
and conductor, b. Munich

A LL new phenomena in music are the work
of genius.   SCHUMANN.

JUNE 12

First performance of Leonard Bernstein's first opera, the one-act, "Trouble in Tahiti," with the composer conducting at Brandeis University (1952)

MUSIC, among those who were styled the chosen people, was a religious art.

ADDISON.

CARLOS CHÁVEZ
Mexican composer and conductor,
b. Mexico City (1899)

PLATO says, that a change in the songs of musicians can change the state of commonwealths.   CICERO.

JUNE 14

BURL IVES
U.S. folksinger, b. Jasper
County, Ill. (1909)

O FTEN as it has been repeated, it is not a mere phrase that music begins where speech ends — provided, of course, that music be content with its proper sphere.

FERDINAND HILLER.

JUNE 15

EDVARD GRIEG
(1843 -1907), Norwegian
composer, b. Bergen

THE sole aim of the composer should be the progress of his art.   GLUCK.

JUNE 16

OTTO JAHN
(1813-1869), German philologist and musicographer,
author of the first critical comparative biography of a
composer (Mozart), b. Kiel

WHENEVER a composer attempts to be a
painter in music, he will succeed in
producing neither good music nor a good
picture.   WAGNER.

IGOR STRAVINSKY
(1882-1971), Russian-American composer
and conductor, b. Oranienbaum near
St. Petersburg

THE value of a work of art consists not in what it conceals or implies, but in what it expresses, and in the mode of expression.

C. M. VON WEBER.

JUNE 18

PAUL McCARTNEY
English rock performer, composer, member of the Beatles,
b. Liverpool (1942)

M USIC has, like society, its laws of propriety
and etiquette ; and even those to whom
their deeper meaning has not been revealed, are
bound to respect and conform to them.

LISZT.

JUNE 19

GUY LOMBARDO
(1902-1977), Canadian-
American bandleader, b.
London, Ontario

BEAUTY of sound is above all rule, as beauty of form is above æsthetics.

SCHUMANN.

JACQUES OFFENBACH
(1819-1880), French operetta
composer (Tales of Hoffman),
b. Cologne

WHATEVER the relations of music, it will never cease to be the noblest and purest of arts. It is the nature of music to bring before us, with absolute truth and reality, what other arts only imply.   WAGNER.

JUNE 21

HERMANN SCHERCHEN
(1891-1966), German con-
ductor, b. Berlin

TO portray passion is not the aim and object of art: it should interpret, not the sensual, but the spiritual.   M. HAUPTMANN.

THE FIRST DAY OF SUMMER

JUNE 22

PETER PEARS
British tenor, b.
Farnham, 1910

A S heart and mind, so do love and art live in
the closest union ; one derives life and
strength from the other.　　　E. T. A. HOFFMANN.

JUNE 23

JAMES LEVINE
U.S. conductor, music director of
the Metropolitan Opera, New York,
b. Cincinnati, Ohio, 1943

A RT and science bind together the best and noblest of men.   BEETHOVEN.

HARRY PARTCH
(1901-1974), U.S. composer
and inventor of instruments,
b. Oakland, Calif.

S IMPLICITY, truth, and unaffectedness are
the leading principles of the beautiful in
every work of art.   GLUCK.

First performance of Igor Stravinsky's ballet,
"L'Oisseau de Feu," Paris (1910)

A RT and composition tolerate no conventional fetters; mind and soul soar above them. HAYDN.

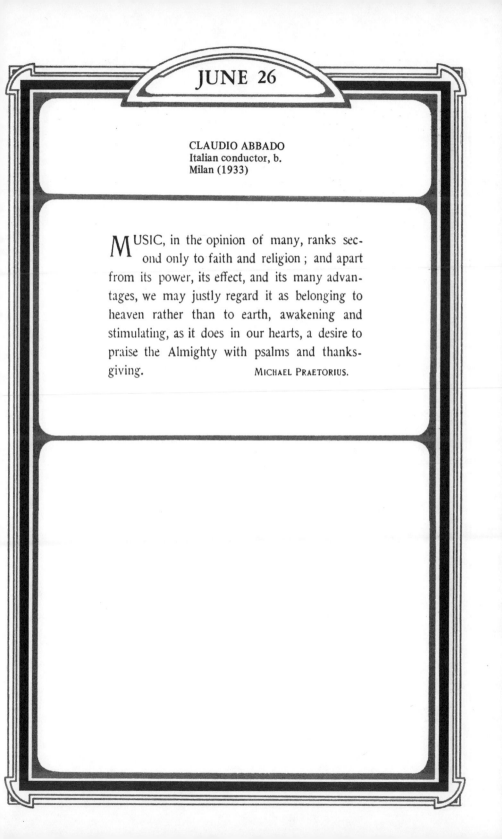

CLAUDIO ABBADO
Italian conductor, b.
Milan (1933)

MUSIC, in the opinion of many, ranks second only to faith and religion ; and apart from its power, its effect, and its many advantages, we may justly regard it as belonging to heaven rather than to earth, awakening and stimulating, as it does in our hearts, a desire to praise the Almighty with psalms and thanksgiving.   MICHAEL PRAETORIUS.

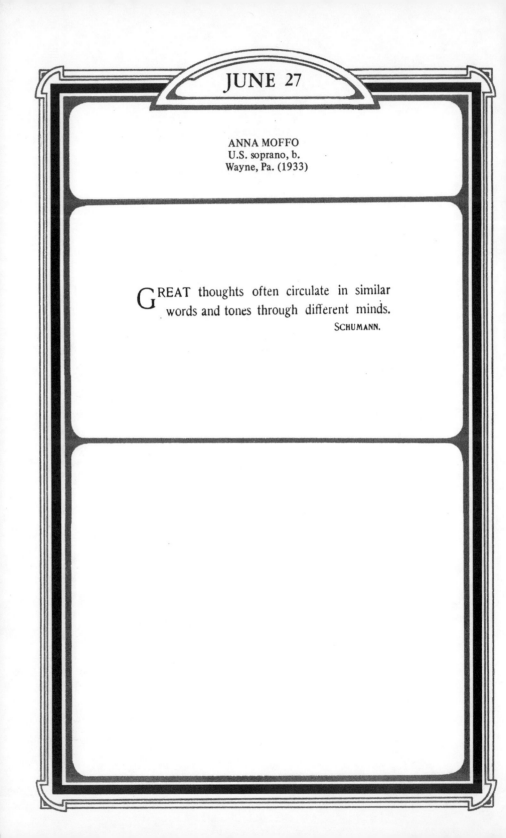

ANNA MOFFO
U.S. soprano, b.
Wayne, Pa. (1933)

GREAT thoughts often circulate in similar words and tones through different minds.

SCHUMANN.

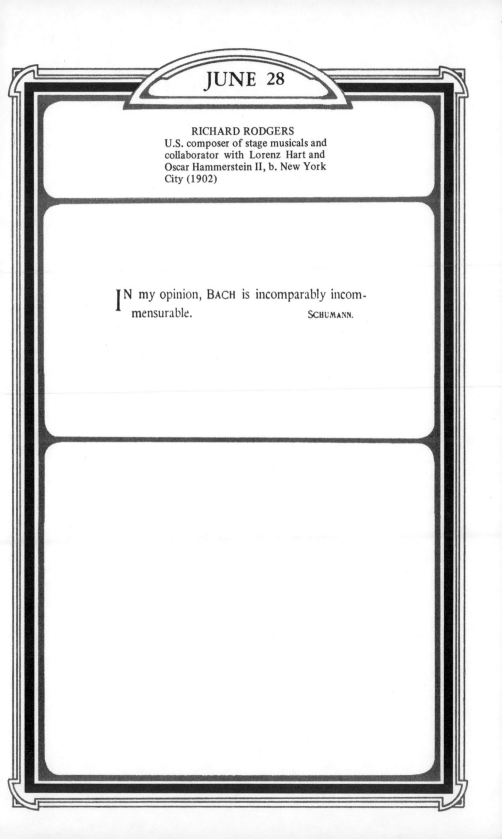

JUNE 28

RICHARD RODGERS
U.S. composer of stage musicals and
collaborator with Lorenz Hart and
Oscar Hammerstein II, b. New York
City (1902)

IN my opinion, BACH is incomparably incommensurable.

SCHUMANN.

JUNE 29

NELSON EDDY
(1901-1967), U.S. popular singer, collaborated
with Jeanette MacDonald in numerous movies,
b. Providence, R.I.

THE first requisite in a musician is, that he should respect, acknowledge, and do homage to what is great and sublime in his art, instead of trying to extinguish the great lights so that his own small one may shine a little more brightly.   MENDELSSOHN.

JUNE 30

LENA HORNE
U.S. popular singer,
b. Brooklyn (1917)

THE more truth and perfection are sought
after, the more necessary are precision and
exactness.   GLUCK.

MENDELSSOHN'S BIRTHPLACE IN HAMBURG

JULY

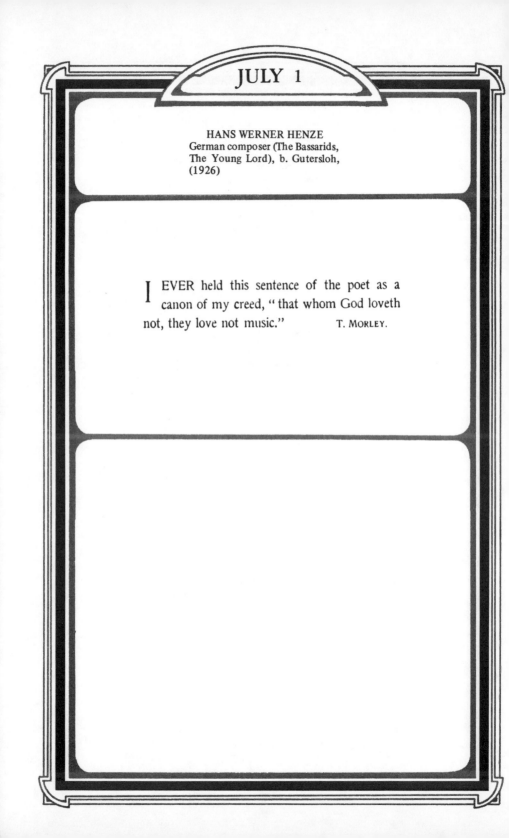

HANS WERNER HENZE
German composer (The Bassarids,
The Young Lord), b. Gutersloh,
(1926)

I EVER held this sentence of the poet as a canon of my creed, "that whom God loveth not, they love not music." T. MORLEY.

CHRISTOPH WILLIBALD GLUCK
(1714 - 1787), opera composer and
reforme, b. Erasbach, Germany

SEE deep enough, and you see musically; the heart of nature being everywhere music, if you can only reach it.   CARLYLE.

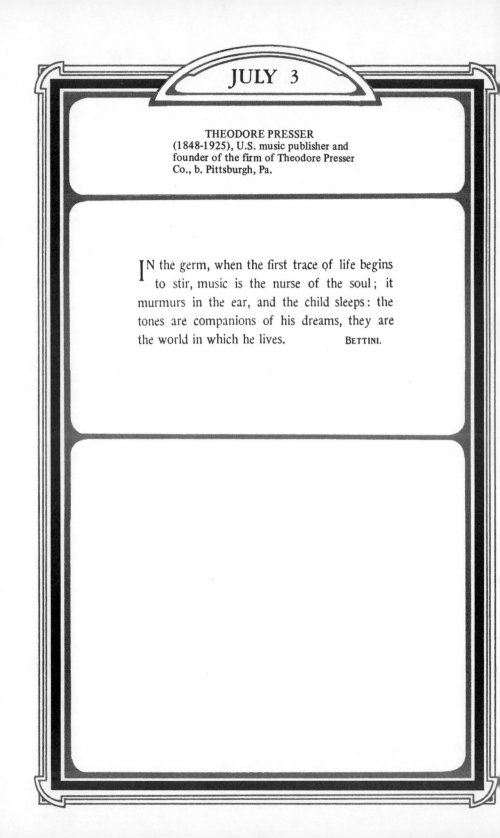

JULY 3

THEODORE PRESSER
(1848-1925), U.S. music publisher and
founder of the firm of Theodore Presser
Co., b. Pittsburgh, Pa.

IN the germ, when the first trace of life begins
to stir, music is the nurse of the soul; it
murmurs in the ear, and the child sleeps: the
tones are companions of his dreams, they are
the world in which he lives.   BETTINI.

JULY 4

LOUIS ("SATCHMO") ARMSTRONG
(1900-1971), U.S. jazz trumpeter, singer,
and bandleader, b. New Orleans

WITHOUT a certain self-sufficiency, talent
cannot accomplish anything really great.

ANON.

INDEPENDENCE DAY

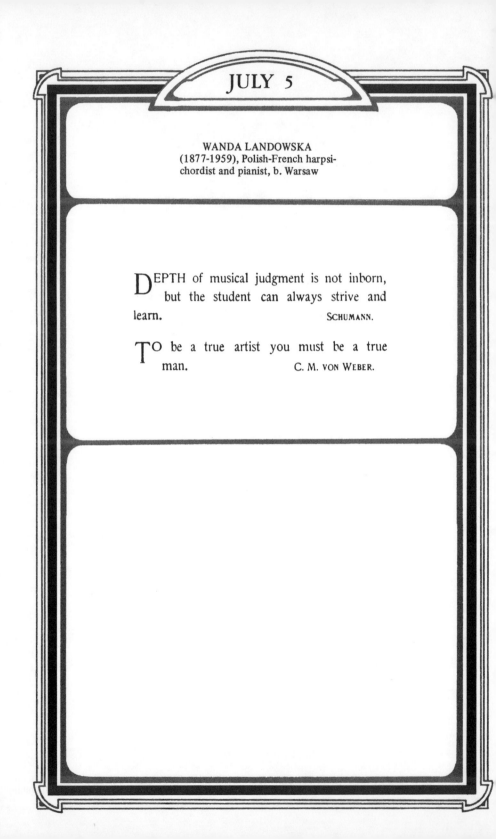

WANDA LANDOWSKA
(1877-1959), Polish-French harpsichordist and pianist, b. Warsaw

DEPTH of musical judgment is not inborn, but the student can always strive and learn.   SCHUMANN.

TO be a true artist you must be a true man.   C. M. VON WEBER.

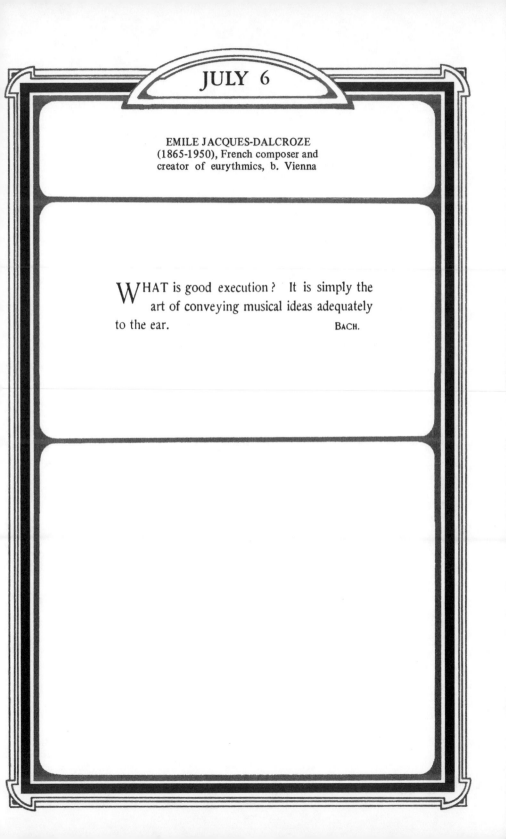

JULY 6

EMILE JACQUES-DALCROZE
(1865-1950), French composer and
creator of eurythmics, b. Vienna

WHAT is good execution? It is simply the
art of conveying musical ideas adequately
to the ear.   BACH.

JULY 7

GUSTAV MAHLER
(1860-1911), Austrian composer and conductor, b. Kal-
ischt, Bohemia

IT is a bird-flight of the soul, when the heart declares itself in song. The affections that clothe themselves with wings are passions that have been subdued to virtues.   SIMMS.

TRUE talent always takes time captive.

SCHUMANN.

JULY 8

PERCY GRAINGER
(1882-1961), Australian-American
pianist and composer, b. Melbourne

A CULTIVATED musician may study Raphael's Madonnas with as much profit as a painter may study Mozart's symphonies.

SCHUMANN.

JULY 9

OTTORINO RESPIGHI
(1879 - 1936), Italian composer
(The Pines of Rome), b. Bologna

THE greatest beauties of melody and harmony
become faults and imperfections, when they
are not in their proper place.   GLUCK.

JULY 10

CARL ORFF
German composer (Carmina
Burana) and music educator,
b. Munich (1895)

OF all fine arts, the most available, universal,
and influential is music.

ALEXANDER BAIN.

THE intellectual realm is the most precious in
my eyes, and far above all temporal and
spiritual monarchies. BEETHOVEN.

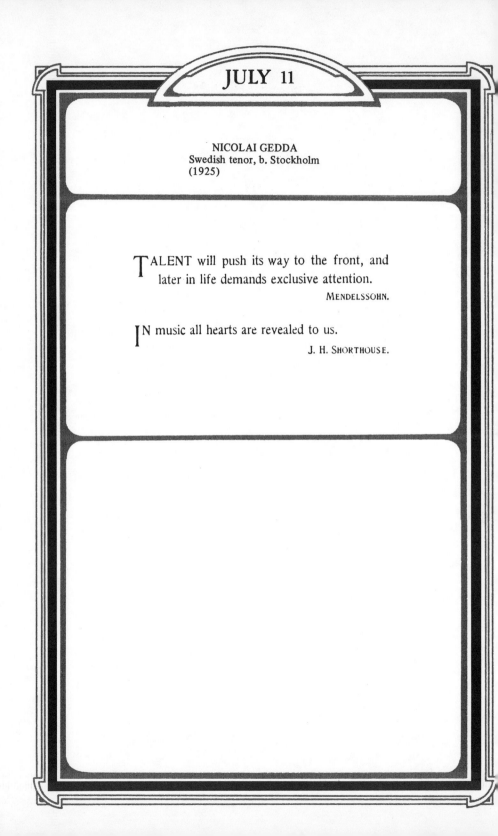

NICOLAI GEDDA
Swedish tenor, b. Stockholm
(1925)

TALENT will push its way to the front, and later in life demands exclusive attention.

MENDELSSOHN.

IN music all hearts are revealed to us.

J. H. SHORTHOUSE.

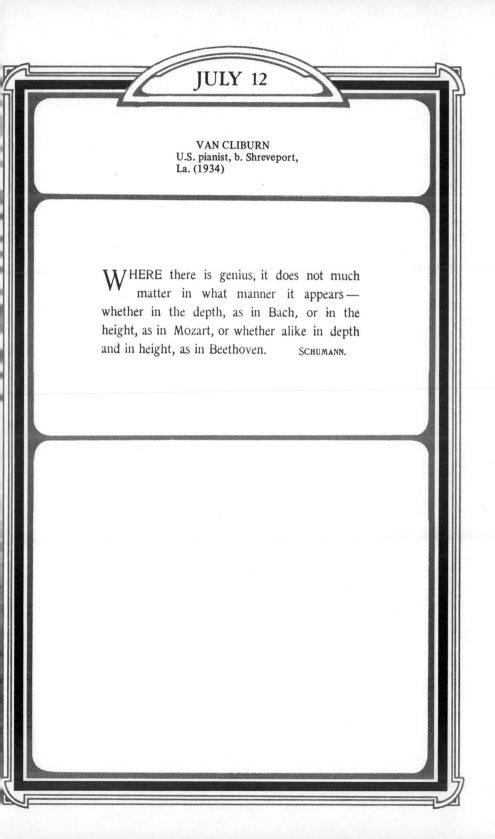

JULY 12

VAN CLIBURN
U.S. pianist, b. Shreveport,
La. (1934)

WHERE there is genius, it does not much matter in what manner it appears — whether in the depth, as in Bach, or in the height, as in Mozart, or whether alike in depth and in height, as in Beethoven.   SCHUMANN.

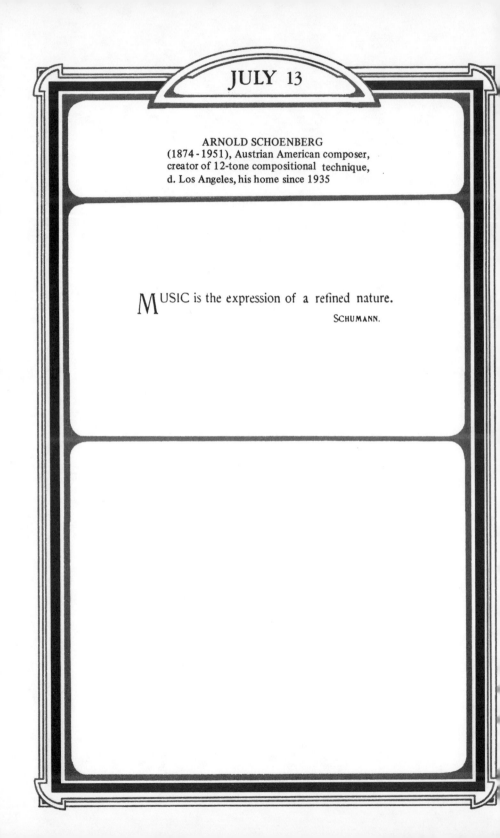

ARNOLD SCHOENBERG
(1874 - 1951), Austrian American composer,
creator of 12-tone compositional technique,
d. Los Angeles, his home since 1935

MUSIC is the expression of a refined nature.

SCHUMANN.

WOODY GUTHRIE
(1912-1967), U.S. folksinger and
composer, b. Okemah, Okla.

PERHAPS the breath of music may prove
more eloquent than my poor words : it is
the medicine of the breaking heart.

ANON.

JACK BEESON
U.S. composer and teacher,
b. Muncie, Indiania (1921)

TO the true artist music should be a necessity,
and not merely an occupation; he should
not manufacture music, he should live in it.

FRANZ.

EUGENE YSAŸE
(1858-1931), Belgian violinist
and conductor, b. Liege

M USIC loosens a heart that care has bound.

BYRD.

JULY 17

SIR DONALD FRANCIS TOVEY
(1875-1940), English conductor and
music scholar, b. Eton

No artist ever began as a master ; and it is
often late in life that the deeper mysteries
of our art are revealed, even to the most gifted.

ANON.

MARIE-AUGUST DURAND
(1830-1909), French organist,
music publisher and founder
of the firm of Durand et Cie.,
b. Paris

G ENIUS is the agency by which the supernatural is revealed to man.   LISZT.

KLAUS EGGE
Norwegian composer,
b. Gransherald (1906)

M USIC exalts each joy, allays each grief,
Expels diseases, softens every pain,
Subdues the rage of poison and of plague.

ANON.

DÉODAT DE SÉVERAC
(1873-1921), French com-
poser b. Laraguais

THE life that is in tune with the melodies of heaven cannot fail of being happy.

J. H. SHORTHOUSE.

JULY 21

HANS BARTH
(1897-1956), German composer and pianist,
registers the patent for a quarter-tone piano
with two keyboards, one tuned to A440, the
other to A427½ (1931)

RICH celestial music thrilled the air
From hosts on hosts of shining ones, who
   thronged
Eastward and Westward, making bright the
   night.   ARNOLD : *Light of Asia.*

LICIA ALBANESE
Italian operatic soprano,
b. Bari (1913)

TO master an art requires a lifetime; and early training is not neglected with impunity.   SCHUMANN.

JULY 23

BEN WEBER
U.S. composer, b. St.
Louis, Mo. (1916)

IN the art of sculpture even a torso is enough to reveal the master; while in music coherence and completeness are indispensable in every individual composition, however small.

SCHUMANN.

JULY 24

ERNEST BLOCH
(1880-1959), Swiss-American composer (Schlelomo), b. Geneva

WHATEVER refines our taste, also refines our feelings. LISZT.

SONG brings of itself a cheerfulness that wakes the heart to joy. EURIPIDES.

ALFREDO CASELLA
(1883-1947), Italian composer,
b. Turin

WHEREVER music unites or amalgamates
with words, it should be to poetry what
the liveliness and brilliancy of color and the
clever and appropriate application of light and
shade are to drawing.   GLUCK.

JULY 26

First performance of Richard Wagner's
"Parsifal" at the Bayreuth Festival of
1882

I LIVE wholly in my music.

BEETHOVEN.

M USIC requires inspiration.

GLUCK.

JULY 27

LEONARD ROSE
U.S. cellist, b. Washington,
D.C. (1918)

S ONG is not only the servant of beauty, but
leads through the beautiful to the good.

ALBERT B. BACH.

JOHANN SEBASTIAN BACH
(1685-1751), d. Leipzig

AT SCHUMANN'S GRAVE.

THY melodies glow with the gracefulness of a noble soul; they shine with the warmth of a loving heart. Quietly listening to the melodious waves of thine own soul, and to all the wonderful harmonies that dwelt there, like flowers of a silent sea, thou wouldst never give way to a frivolous vanity, which tempts an artist's soul too often with seductive chords and melodies.

FERDINAND HILLER.

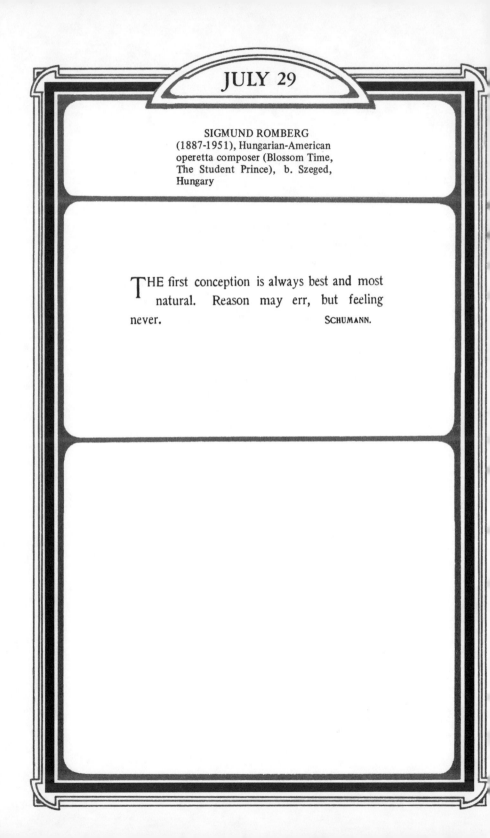

SIGMUND ROMBERG
(1887-1951), Hungarian-American
operetta composer (Blossom Time,
The Student Prince), b. Szeged,
Hungary

THE first conception is always best and most natural. Reason may err, but feeling never. SCHUMANN.

JULY 30

PAUL ANKA
Canadian songwriter
and entertainer, b.
Ottawa (1941)

MUSIC, the daughter rather than the imitator of Nature, impelling us to pious thought by its solemn, mysterious accents, appeals directly to our feelings, and is mistress of our deepest emotions.   C. M. VON WEBER.

FRANZ LISZT'S playing often seems to me like a melodious agony of the spectre-world.   HEINE.

JULY 31

PERCY SCHOLES
(1877 - 1958), English musical scholar
and lexicographer (Oxford Companion
to Music), d. Vevey, Switzerland

MY idea is, that music ought to move the heart with sweet emotion, which a pianist will never effect by mere scrambling, thundering, and arpeggios — at least not from me. BACH.

AUGUST

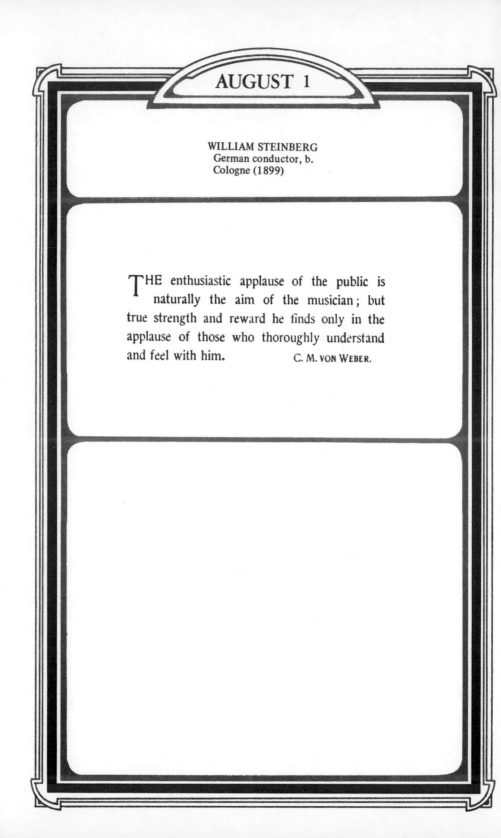

WILLIAM STEINBERG
German conductor, b.
Cologne (1899)

THE enthusiastic applause of the public is naturally the aim of the musician; but true strength and reward he finds only in the applause of those who thoroughly understand and feel with him.   C. M. VON WEBER.

SIR ARTHUR BLISS
(1891-1975), English composer,
b. London

THE unbounded universe is one sleepless lyre,
whose chords of love, of hope, of purity
and peace are fanned into a dreamy and mystic
melody by the breath of the invisible God.

ANON.

AUGUST 3

LOUIS GRUENBERG
(1884-1964), U.S. composer
(The Emperor Jones), b. near
Brest Litovsk, Poland

M USIC should strike fire from the heart of man and bring tears from the eyes of woman. BEETHOVEN.

AUGUST 4

WILLIAM SCHUMAN
U.S. composer, former president
of the Julliard School, b. New
York City (1910)

M USIC crept by me upon the waters,
   Allaying both their fury and my passion
With its sweet air.   SHAKESPEARE.

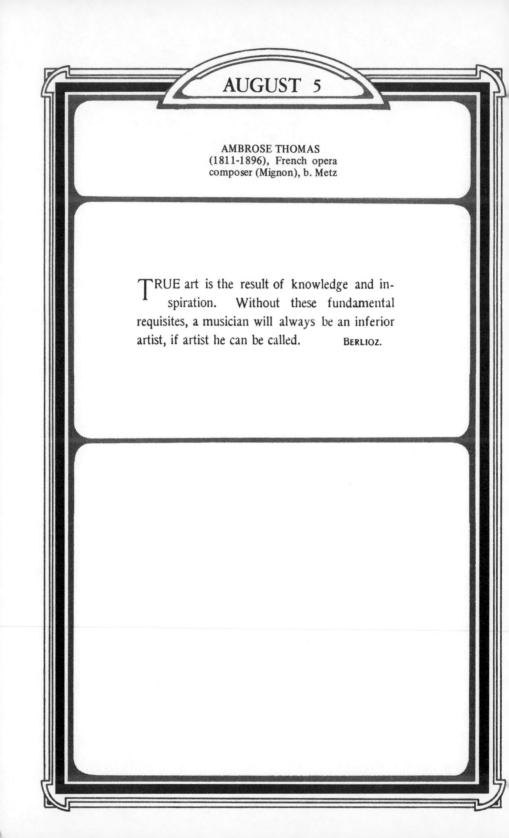

AMBROSE THOMAS
(1811-1896), French opera
composer (Mignon), b. Metz

TRUE art is the result of knowledge and inspiration. Without these fundamental requisites, a musician will always be an inferior artist, if artist he can be called. BERLIOZ.

AUGUST 6

The first "100% sound motion picture," "Don Juan," made by the Vitaphone Company, featuring the composer Henry Hadley and the N.Y. Philharmonic, opens at the Warner Theater, N.Y.C. (1926)

EXPLAIN it as we may, a martial strain will urge a man into the front rank of battle sooner than an argument, and a fine anthem excite his devotion more certainly than a logical discourse. TUCKERMAN.

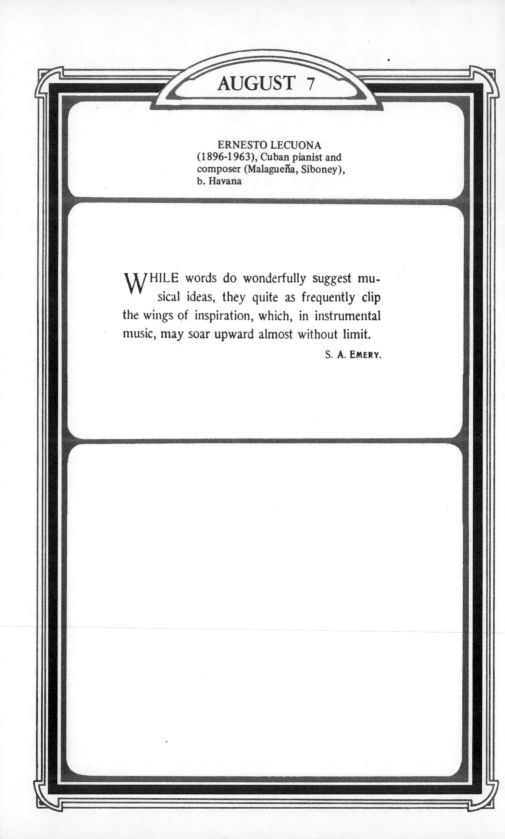

ERNESTO LECUONA
(1896-1963), Cuban pianist and
composer (Malagueña, Siboney),
b. Havana

WHILE words do wonderfully suggest musical ideas, they quite as frequently clip
the wings of inspiration, which, in instrumental
music, may soar upward almost without limit.

S. A. EMERY.

AUGUST 8

ANDRÉ JOLIVET
(1905-1975), French pianist, composer
and conductor, b. Paris

A ND what is our failure here but a triumph's
evidence
For the fulness of the days? Have we withered
or agonized?
Why else was the pause prolonged, but that
singing might issue thence?
Why rushed the discords in, but that harmony
should be prized?   ROBERT BROWNING.

JOHN DRYDEN
(1631-1700), English poet and librettist
for Henry Purcell (King Arthur, Ode to
Saint Cecilia), b. Northamptonshire

TO be a skilful artist, one must be naturally endowed with a strong reason, fully trained and developed for the work at hand; but for such a development, the study of music alone would prove wholly inadequate.

S. A. EMERY.

AUGUST 10

DOUGLAS MOORE
(1893-1969), U.S. composer (The
Ballad of Baby Doe) and teacher,
b. Cutchogue, N.Y.

TRUE, it must be the leading pursuit for the professional musician; but it must be as a noble river: though small and unobserved in its source, winding at first alone its tortuous way through opposing obstacles, yet ever broadening and deepening, fed by countless streams on either hand, till it rolls onward in a mighty sweep, at once a glory and a blessing to the earth.   S. A. EMERY.

The International Society for Contemporary Music
is organized in Salzburg, Austria, with Edward J.
Dent as president (1922)

THERE can be nothing more barren in the
world than one idea, springing from one
idea, nourished on one idea, and aiming at one
idea : and there can be nothing weaker than a
conglomeration of countless ideas, having no
common centre, not even self-supporting, much
less supporting aught else.   S. A. EMERY.

AUGUST 12

GIOVANNI GABRIELI
(c. 1554-1612), Italian organist
and celebrated polychoral composer, d. Venice

IT is indispensable, therefore, that the musician
make music his central point ; and equally
indispensable that he have, as supports to this,
knowledge and theories drawn from a thousand
sources. S. A. EMERY.

AUGUST 13

SIR GEORGE GROVE
(1820-1900), musical encyclopedist, first
director of the Royal College of Music, b.
London

REGARD it as something abominable to meddle with the pieces of good writers either by alteration, omission, or by the introduction of new-fangled ornaments. This is the greatest indignity you can inflict on art.

SCHUMANN.

AUGUST 14

The first musical broadcast via satelite is made
when "America the Beautiful'. is transmitted
through Echo I from New Jersey to California
(1960)

OFTEN have I said from my very soul with
Luther, and will here say again, " Music
is a fair and glorious gift of God.   I would not
for the world forgo my humble share of it."

THIBAUT.

LUKAS FOSS
U.S. composer and conductor,
b. Berlin (1922)

M USIC waves eternal wands,
Enchantress of the souls of mortals.

E. C. STEDMAN.

AUGUST 16

GABRIEL PIERNÉ
(1863-1937), French composer
and conductor, b. Metz

M USIC wakes a glad remembrance of our
youth, calls back past joys, and warms us
into transport.   ROWE.

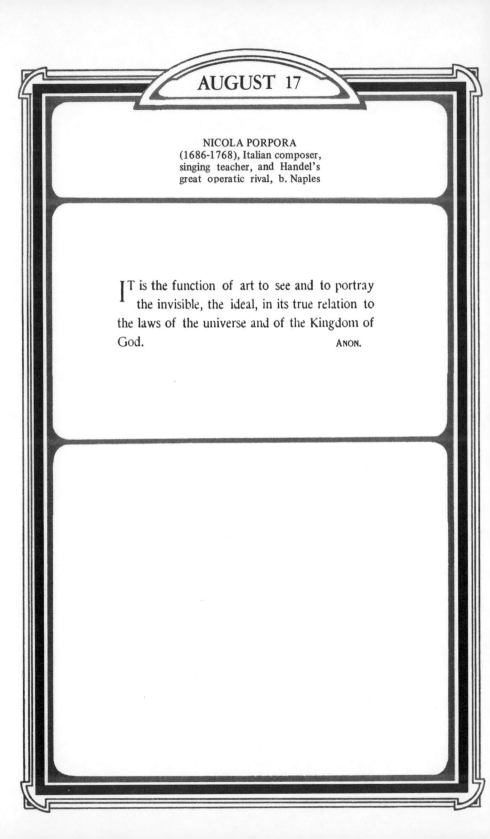

AUGUST 17

NICOLA PORPORA
(1686-1768), Italian composer,
singing teacher, and Handel's
great operatic rival, b. Naples

I T is the function of art to see and to portray
the invisible, the ideal, in its true relation to
the laws of the universe and of the Kingdom of
God.   ANON.

AUGUST 18

ANTONIA SALIERA
(1750-1825), composer, teacher (of Beethoven, Schubert, et
al), and great rival of Mozart,
b. Legnano

THERE is something sacramental in perfect metre and rhythm. They are outward and visible signs of an inward and spiritual grace; namely, of the self-possessed and victorious touches of one who has so far subdued nature as to be able to hear that universal sphere-music of hers, speaking of which Mr. Carlyle says that " All deepest thoughts instinctively vent themselves in song." CHARLES KINGSLEY.

AUGUST 19

GEORGES ENESCO
(1881-1955), Rumanian composer and violinist, b. Liveni

ALL inmost things, we may say, are melodious; naturally utter themselves in song. The meaning of song goes deep.

CARLYLE.

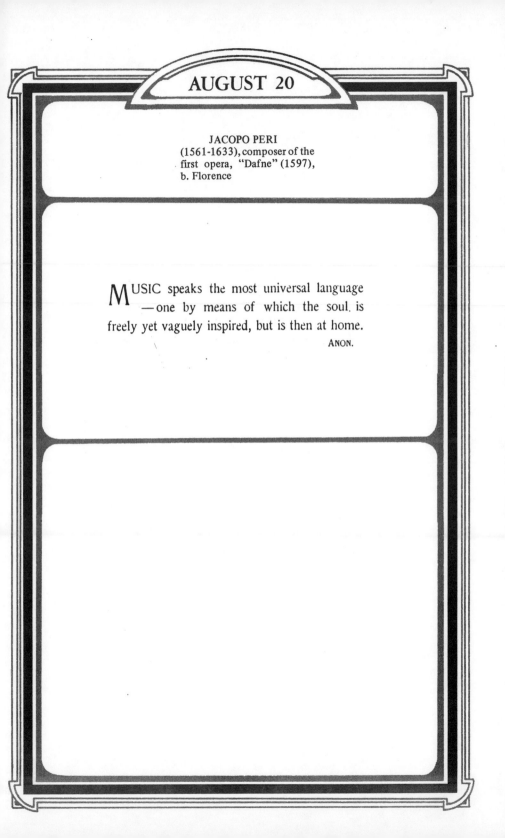

AUGUST 20

JACOPO PERI
(1561-1633), composer of the
first opera, "Dafne" (1597),
b. Florence

MUSIC speaks the most universal language
—one by means of which the soul. is
freely yet vaguely inspired, but is then at home.

ANON.

AUGUST 21

WILLIAM ("COUNT") BASIE
U.S. jazz pianist, composer and
band leader, b. Red Bank, N.J.
(1904)

THERE is music in heaven because there is no
self-will. Music goes on certain laws and
rules; man did not make the laws of music,
he has only found them out; and if he be self-
willed and break them, there is an end of music
instantly.   ANON.

CLAUDE DEBUSSY
(1862-1918), French composer,
b. St. Germain-en-laye

M USIC unites mankind by an ideal bond.

WAGNER.

CONSTANT LAMBERT
English composer, conductor
and critic, b. London (1905)

THE pleasure which the work of a musician
affords you is his very life-blood; the
trouble it has cost him you do not know. He
gives you his very best — the essence of his
life, the outflow of his genius; and yet you
grudge him a simple wreath of flowers.

SCHUMANN.

AUGUST 24

THEODORE DUBOIS
(1837-1924), French organist and
composer, b. Rosnay, Marne

S TRANGE! that a harp of thousand strings
Should keep in tune so long.   WATTS.

O SECRET music! sacred tongue of God!
I hear thee calling to me, and I come!
LELAND: *The Music Lesson of Confucius.*

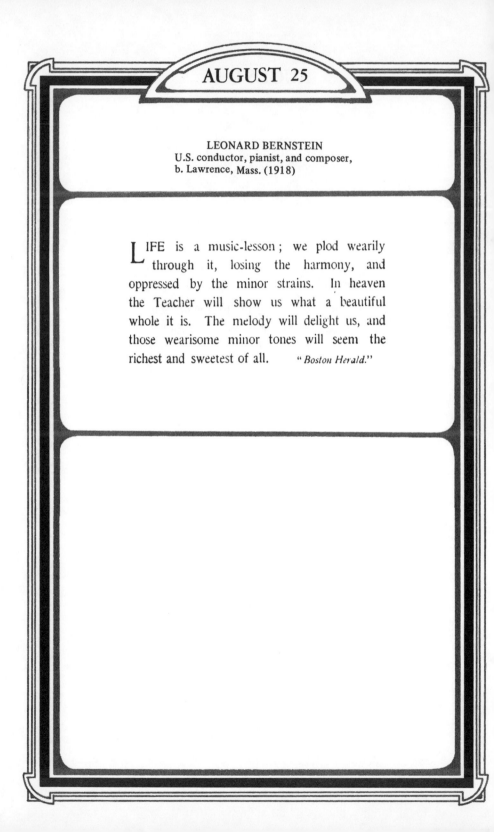

LEONARD BERNSTEIN
U.S. conductor, pianist, and composer,
b. Lawrence, Mass. (1918)

LIFE is a music-lesson; we plod wearily through it, losing the harmony, and oppressed by the minor strains. In heaven the Teacher will show us what a beautiful whole it is. The melody will delight us, and those wearisome minor tones will seem the richest and sweetest of all. *"Boston Herald."*

AUGUST 26

First performance of Felix Mendelssohn's oratorio,
"Elijah," Birmingham, England (1846)

THE future mission of music for the millions
is the discipline of the emotions.

HAWEIS.

JOSQUIN DES PREZ
(c.1440-1521), greatest of the
Renaissance Franco-Flemish
composers, d. Hainault, Bur-
gundy

GOD is its author, and not man, — He laid
　　The keynote of all harmonies, He planned
All perfect combinations, and He made
Us so that we could hear and understand.

ANON.

AUGUST 28

RICHARD TUCKER
(1913-1975), U.S. lyric tenor,
b. Brooklyn, N.Y.

S WEETEST the strains when in the song the singer has been lost.

ELIZABETH STUART PHELPS.

M USIC when thus applied raises in the mind of the hearers great conceptions. It strengthens devotion, and advances praise into rapture.

ADDISON.

AUGUST 29

CHARLIE ("BYRD") PARKER
(1920-1955), U.S. jazz saxophonist
and composer, b. Kansas City, Mo.

A ND wheresoever in his rich creation,
   Sweet music breathes in wave or bird or
     soul,
'T is but the faint and far reverberation
Of that great tune to which the planets roll.

FRANCIS S. OSGOOD.

PERCY GOETSCHIUS
(1853-1943), U.S. pedagogue
and theorist, b. Patterson, N.J.

IT is by pictures and music, by art and sound
. . . that all nations have been educated in
their adolescence.   KINGSLEY.

AUGUST 31

First performance of Kurt Weill's "Die Dreigroschenoper" The Three-penny Opera), Berlin (1928)

THE combination of the arts must be sought for within the depths of the soul, but as they do not all speak the same language, they can only be affected by, and explain themselves to each other, through the most mysterious analogies, in which, after all, each one only explains itself.   GEORGES SAND.

SEPTEMBER

ROSH HASHANA

1979	September 22
1980	September 11
1981	September 29
1982	September 18
1983	September 8
1984	September 27
1985	September 16
1986	October 4
1987	September 24

LABOR DAY: The first Monday

ENGELBERT HUMPERDINCK
(1854-1921), German composer
(Hansel and Gretel), b. Siegburg,
near Bonn

LIFE'S KEY.

THE hand that fashioned me tuned my ear
    To chord with the major key ;
In the darkest moments of life I hear
Strains of courage, and hope and cheer
From choirs that I cannot see ;
And the music of life seems so inspired
That it will not let me grow sad or tired.

ELLA WHEELER WILCOX.

FRANCESCO LANDINI
(1325-1397), great Italian
"Ars Nova"composer and
organist, d. Florence

YET through and under the magic strain
  I hear, with the passing of years,
The mournful minor's measures of pain,
Of souls that struggle and toil in vain
For a goal that never nears ;
And the sorrowful cadence of good gone wrong
Breaks more and more into earth's glad song.

ELLA WHEELER WILCOX.

SEPTEMBER 3

ADRIANO BANCHIERI
(1568-1634), Italian organist,
stage and madrigal composer,
b. Bologna

A ND oft, in the dark of the night, I wake
   And think of sorrowing lives;
And I long to comfort the hearts that ache,
To sweeten the cup that is bitter to take,
And to strengthen each soul that strives.
I long to cry to them : "Do not fear!
Help is coming and aid is near."

ELLA WHEELER WILCOX.

ANTON BRUCKNER
(1824-1896), Austrian
composer, b. Ansfelden

H OWEVER desolate, weird, or strange
Life's monody sounds to you,
Before to-morrow the air may change,
And the Great Director of music arrange
A programme perfectly new ;
And the dirge in minor may suddenly be
Turned into a jubilant song of glee.

ELLA WHEELER WILCOX.

SEPTEMBER 5

JOHN CAGE
U.S. experimental composer,
b. Los Angeles (1912)

NATURE is not a dead repository of facts. It is a living keyboard for the imagination to play upon, out of which infinite combinations of harmony or melody may be produced.

ANON.

SEPTEMBER 6

VINCENT NOVELLO
(1781-1861), organist, composer, founder
of the English music publishing house, Novello & Co., b. London

FOR a man to comprehend a work of genius,
he must certainly possess some power cor-
relative to that power who created it.

APTHORP.

SEPTEMBER 7

THOMAS WHITNEY SURETTE
(1861-1941), U.S. composer and
music educator, b. Concord, Mass.

WE can give no better advice to any who study the pianoforte earnestly, than that they should study and learn practically the beautiful art of singing.   THALBERG.

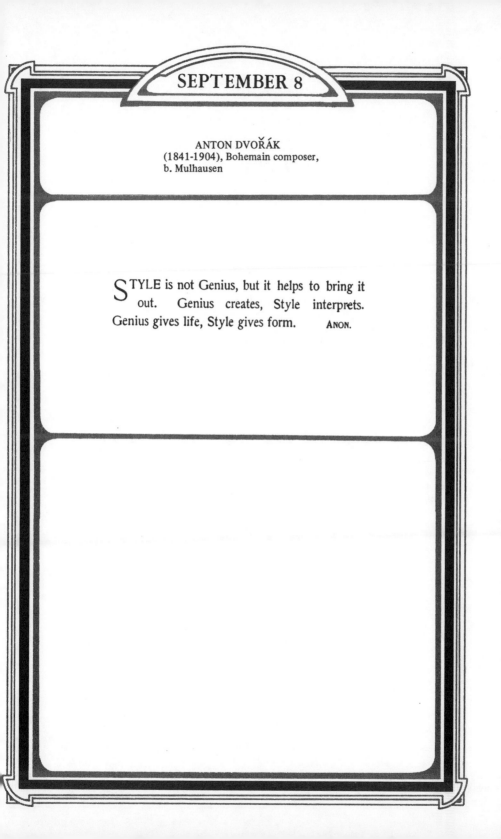

SEPTEMBER 8

ANTON DVOŘÁK
(1841-1904), Bohemain composer,
b. Mulhausen

STYLE is not Genius, but it helps to bring it out. Genius creates, Style interprets. Genius gives life, Style gives form. ANON.

SEPTEMBER 9

EDWARD BURLINGHAME HILL
(1872-1960), U.S. composer, b.
Cambridge, Mass.

O F all the arts beneath the heaven
    That man has found or God has given,
None draws the soul so sweet away
As music's melting mystic lay ;
Slight emblem of the bliss above,
It soothes the spirit all to love.

JAMES HOGG.

YMA SUMAC
Peruvian-American singer with
astoninsingly wide vocal range,
b. Ichocan (1927)

A CHORD of love runs through all the sounds of creation; but the ear of love alone can distinguish it.　　　ANON.

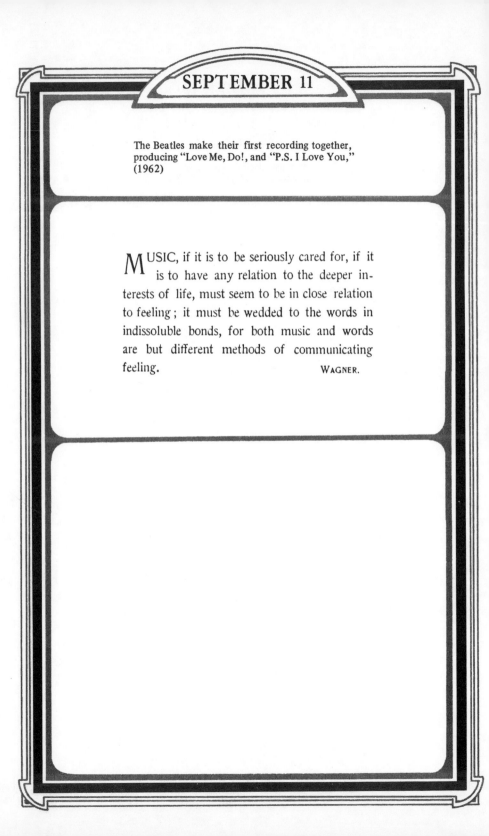

The Beatles make their first recording together, producing "Love Me, Do!, and "P.S. I Love You," (1962)

M USIC, if it is to be seriously cared for, if it is to have any relation to the deeper interests of life, must seem to be in close relation to feeling; it must be wedded to the words in indissoluble bonds, for both music and words are but different methods of communicating feeling.   WAGNER.

SEPTEMBER 12

BENJAMIN CARR
(176801831), pioneer U.S.
compo ser and publisher, the
first to issue American compositions, b. London

I CAN grasp the spirit of music in no .other manner than in love.   WAGNER.

SEPTEMBER 13

ARNOLD SCHOENBERG
(1874-1951), Austrian-American
composer, developer of the 12-
tone serial technique of composition, b. Vienna

OBSERVE how all passionate language does of itself become musical, with a finer music than the mere accent; the speech of man, even in zealous anger, becomes a chant — a song; all deep things are song.

CARLYLE.

LEHMAN ENGEL
U.S. conductor, composer and
writer, b. Jackson, Miss. (1910)

A S Beethoven regarded his art as something sacred, which he placed higher than all philosophy, so must a refined artist possess an innate horror of all vulgar, frivolous, and effeminate music.   ANON.

SEPTEMBER 15

BRUNO WALTER
(1876-1962), German-American conductor,
friend and champion of Gustav Mahler, b.
Berlin

TRUE art, therefore, brings us in contact with the Divine idea, and in this sense all true art must be sacred.   SCHOPENHAUER.

NADIA BOULANGER
French conductor and influential teacher
(of Walter Piston, Aaron Copland, Virgil
Thomson, et al), b. Paris (1887)

M ELODY tells the most secret emotions of
the heart, and reveals every desire of the
human will; hence it is called the language of
emotions.   SCHOPENHAUER.

SEPTEMBER 17

CHARLES GRIFFES
(1884-1920), U.S. impressionistic composer
(The Pleasure Dome of Kubla Khan), b. El-
mira, N.Y.

HE who has once learned the self-control of the musician, the use of piano and forte, each in its right place, when to be lightly swift or majestically slow, and especially how to keep to the key once chosen, until the right time has come for changing it ; he who has once learned this, knows the secrets of the art.

P. G. HAMERTON.

SEPTEMBER 18

GERLAD TYRWHITT, LORD BERNERS
(1883-1950), British diplomat and composer,
b. Arley Park, Bridgenorth

L OVE took up the harp of life, and smote on
all the chords with might ;
Smote the chord of self, that trembling, passed
in music out of sight.   TENNYSON.

GUSTAV SCHIRMER
(1929-1893), founder of the
New York music publishing
house of G. Schirmer, Inc.,
b. Thuringia

S TRICTLY instrumental music, such as our great masters have bequeathed to the world in their symphonies, quartets, and sonatas, is, perhaps, the only artistic production in which the Germans stand alone. There is no branch of the Art which, in order to be correctly and completely understood, demands from the listener greater attention and devotion.

FERDINAND HILLER.

"JELLY ROLL" MORTON
(1885-1941), U.S. jazz pianist,
composer, and band leader, b.
Gulfport, La.

YOU do poets and their song
    A grievous wrong,
If your own heart does not bring
To their deep imagining
As much beauty as they sing.

T. B. ALDRICH.

FRANCIS HOPKINSON
(1737-1791), U.S. statesman, signer of the
Declaration of Independence, first native
American composer, b. Philadelphia

IT is a pity that it is impossible to acquire
musical culture as easily as reading and writing ; for the pleasure of diving into the depths
and beauties of the score of a masterwork is as
great and intense a pleasure as any in the whole
range of art. SCHUMANN.

SEPTEMBER 22

First performance of Richard Wagner's "Das Rheingold,"
the introduction to his tetralogy, "Der Ring des Nibelung-
en," Munich (1869)

A N artist who always moves in the same style
and groove, becomes in the end a pedant
and mannerist: and nothing does him more
harm than to content himself too long with a
given style, simply because it is convenient.

SCHUMANN.

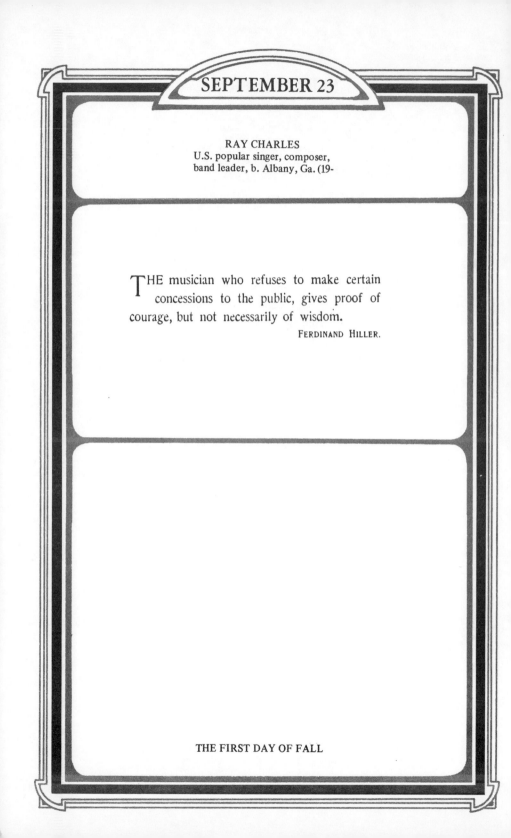

SEPTEMBER 23

RAY CHARLES
U.S. popular singer, composer,
band leader, b. Albany, Ga. (19-

THE musician who refuses to make certain concessions to the public, gives proof of courage, but not necessarily of wisdom.

FERDINAND HILLER.

THE FIRST DAY OF FALL

SEPTEMBER 24

JAMES A. BLAND
(1854-1911), U.S. minstrel performer
and songwriter (Carry Me Back to Old
Virginny), b. Flushing, N.Y.

'TIS God gives skill,
But not without men's hands: we could
not make
Antonio Stradivari's violins without Antonio.

GEORGE ELIOT.

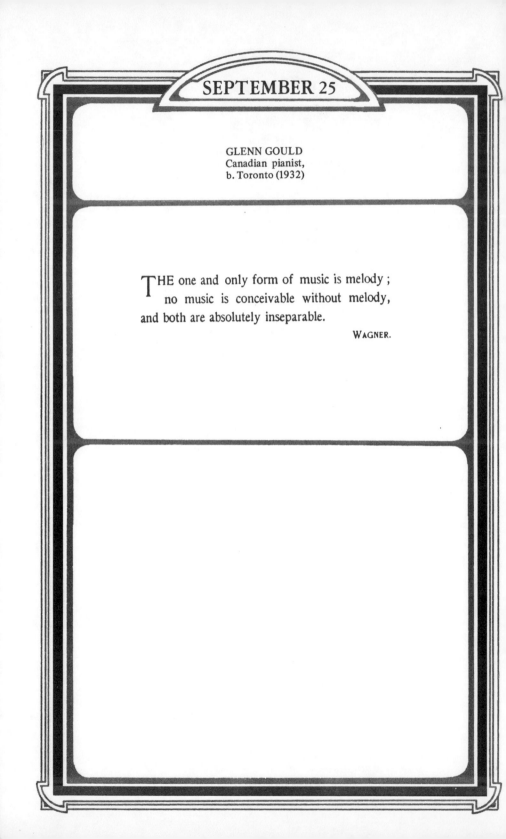

SEPTEMBER 25

GLENN GOULD
Canadian pianist,
b. Toronto (1932)

THE one and only form of music is melody ;
no music is conceivable without melody,
and both are absolutely inseparable.

WAGNER.

SEPTEMBER 26

GEORGE GERSHWIN
(1898-1937), U.S. pianist and
composer, b. Brooklyn, N.Y.

M USIC is love in search of a word.

S. LANIER.

SEPTEMBER 27

EARL ("BUD") POWELL
(1924-1966), U.S. jazz pianist and
composer, b. New York City

H^E makes sweet music with the enamel'd
stones,
Giving a gentle kiss to every sedge
He overtaketh in his pilgrimage.

SHAKESPEARE.

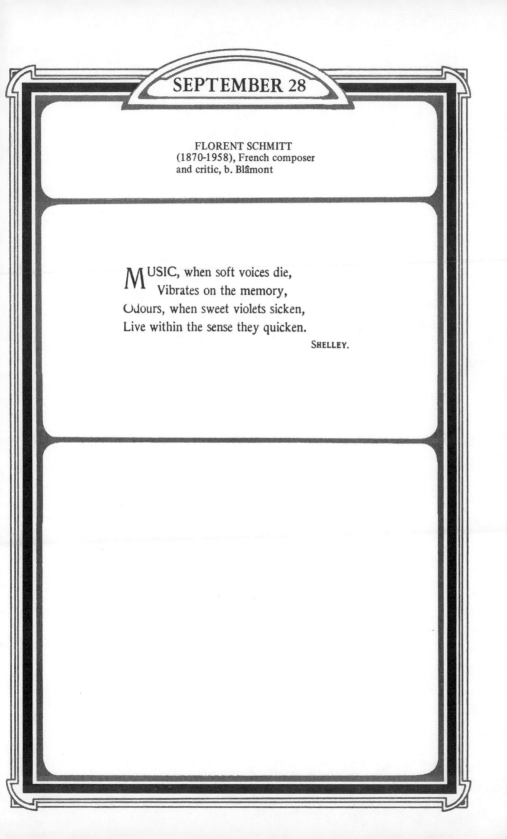

SEPTEMBER 28

FLORENT SCHMITT
(1870-1958), French composer
and critic, b. Blâmont

M USIC, when soft voices die,
     Vibrates on the memory,
Odours, when sweet violets sicken,
Live within the sense they quicken.

SHELLEY.

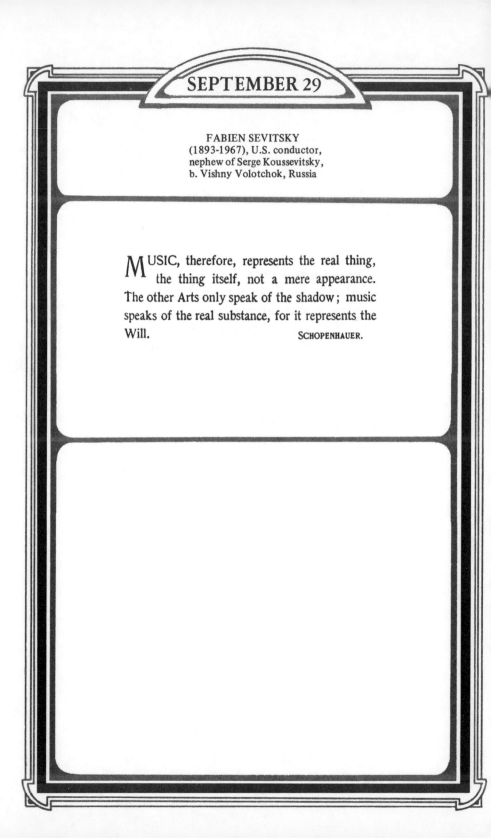

FABIEN SEVITSKY
(1893-1967), U.S. conductor,
nephew of Serge Koussevitsky,
b. Vishny Volotchok, Russia

MUSIC, therefore, represents the real thing, the thing itself, not a mere appearance. The other Arts only speak of the shadow; music speaks of the real substance, for it represents the Will.   SCHOPENHAUER.

The first performance of George Gershwin's "Porgy and Bess," his last major work, in Boston (1935)

GOOD music expresses pure emotions, and for this reason it will eventually pass around the world and remain true forever.

SCHOPENHAUER.

BEETHOVEN'S BIRTHPLACE IN BONN

OCTOBER

YOM KIPPUR
1979	October 1
1980	September 20
1981	October 8
1982	September 27
1983	September 17
1984	October 6
1985	September 25
1986	October 13
1987	October 3

VLADIMIR HOROWITZ
Russian-American pianist,
b. Kiev (1904)

M USIC is the best limner of affections, and
the very worst of material objects.

A. W. AMBROS.

OCTOBER 2

HENRY CLAY WORK
(1832-1884), U.S. songwriter
(Marching through Georgia ,
Kingdom Coming), b. Middle-
town, Conn.

THE habitual use of vocal music by a family
is an almost unfailing sign of good morals
and refined taste.   C. W. LANDON.

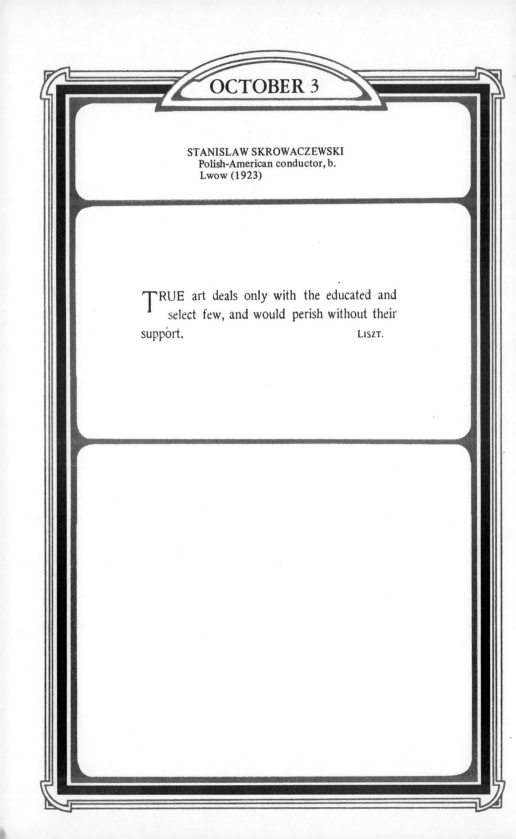

STANISLAW SKROWACZEWSKI
Polish-American conductor, b.
Lwow (1923)

TRUE art deals only with the educated and select few, and would perish without their support.   LISZT.

OCTOBER 4

The American Academy in Rome is founded, and the first fellowship in musical composition is awarded to Leo Sowerby (1921)

WHICH of the two powers is able to raise men to the highest spheres — love, or music ? . . , I think we may say, that while love can give us no idea of music, music can realize the idea of love.   But why separate one from the other ?   The soul soars on the wings of both.   BERLIOZ.

First performance of the original version of Christoph Willibald Gluck's opera, "Orfeo ed Euridice," Vienna (1762)

S INGING is one preparation for heaven.

BEVAN.

OCTOBER 6

JENNY LIND
(1820-1887), Swedish soprano,
b. Stockholm

WHAT a marvellous thing is music! How little are we able to fathom its deep mysteries! And yet, does it not live in the very heart of man? Does it not so imbue him with its grace and beauty, that his mind is wholly engrossed by it; that another and purer life seems to raise him above the shallows and miseries here on earth?

ERNST THEODOR HOFFMANN.

WILLIAM BILLINGS
(1746-1800), pioneer U.S. composer,
foremost proponent of "the fuging
tune," b. Boston

THE more of pains the artist takes,
The more with diligence he strives,
So much the more his purpose thrives.
Then *practice* every day ; you 'll see
What the result of this will be.
For thus is every aim attained,
What 's hard at first with ease is gained,
Until at length your very hand
Itself appears to understand.   GOETHE.

OCTOBER 8

HEINRICH SCHÜTZ
(1585-1672), German composer and eminent teacher, one of the earliest to develop the Baroque style in northern Europe, b. Köstritz

A GOOD ear for music, and a taste for music, are two very different things, which are often confounded; and so is comprehending and enjoying every object of sense and sentiment. GREVILLE.

OCTOBER 9

JOHN LENNON
English rock performer, composer, member of the Beatles,
b. Liverpool (1940)

THERE is no music in a rest, but there is the making of music in it. In our whole life-melody the music is broken off here and there by " rests," and we foolishly think we have come to the end of the tune.   RUSKIN.

OCTOBER 10

GIUSEPPE VERDI
(1813-1901), Italian composer,
b. Le Roncole, Parma

G OD sends a time of forced leisure, sickness, disappointed plans, frustrated efforts, and makes a sudden pause in the choral hymn of our lives, and we lament that our voices must be silent and our part missing in the music which ever goes up to the ear of the Creator.

RUSKIN.

OCTOBER 11

THEODORE THOMAS
(1835-1905), German-American
conductor, founder of the Chicago Symphony (1891), b. East
Friesland

S EE him beat the time with unwavering count
and catch up the next note as if no break
had come between.   Not without design does
God write the music of our lives.   RUSKIN.

LUCIANO PAVAROTTI
Italian tenor, b. Modena
(1936)

B^E it ours to learn the tune and not be dismayed at the "rests." They are not to be omitted. If we look up, God himself will beat the time for us. With the eye on Him we shall strike the next note full and clear.   RUSKIN.

OCTOBER 13

HUGO WEISGALL
U.S. serial composer, b.
Czechoslovakia (1912)

THERE is nothing that I can tell you with more eager desire that you should believe, nothing with wider grounds in my experience for requiring you to believe, than this, that you never will love art well till you love what she mirrors better.   RUSKIN.

OCTOBER 14

GARY GRAFFMAN
U.S. pianist, b. New York City
(1928)

H OW soft the music of those village bells,
   Falling at intervals upon the ear
In cadence sweet !   COWPER.

M USIC was taught to Achilles in order to
   moderate his passions.   HOMER.

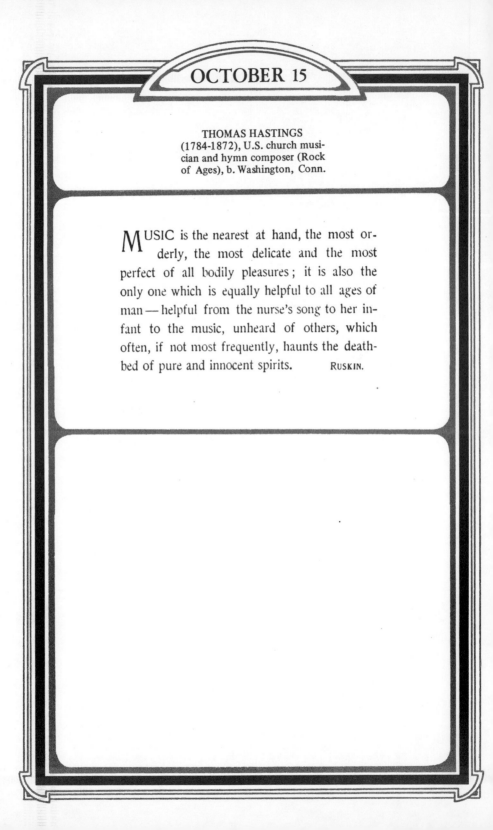

OCTOBER 15

THOMAS HASTINGS
(1784-1872), U.S. church musician and hymn composer (Rock of Ages), b. Washington, Conn.

MUSIC is the nearest at hand, the most orderly, the most delicate and the most perfect of all bodily pleasures; it is also the only one which is equally helpful to all ages of man — helpful from the nurse's song to her infant to the music, unheard of others, which often, if not most frequently, haunts the deathbed of pure and innocent spirits.   RUSKIN.

OCTOBER 16

First performance of Arnold Schoenberg's
song cycle, "Pierrot Lunaire," Berlin (1912)

A ND the night shall be filled with music,
  And the cares that infest the day
Shall fold their tents, like the Arabs,
And as silently steal away.   LONGFELLOW.

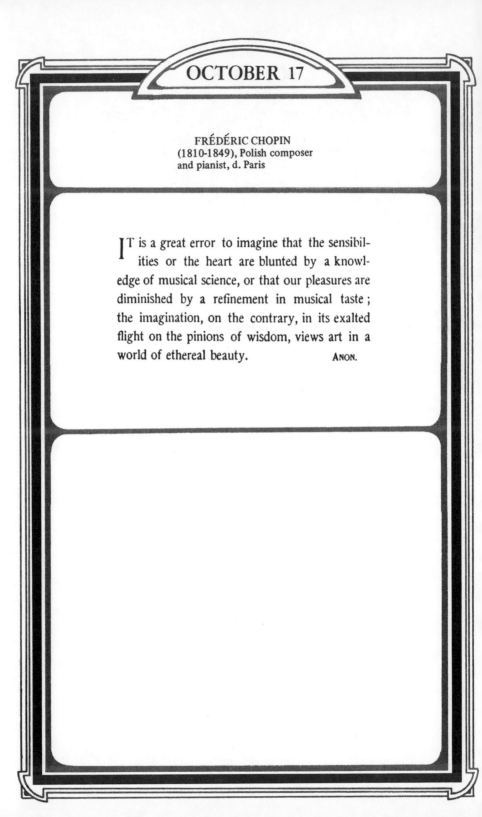

OCTOBER 17

FRÉDÉRIC CHOPIN
(1810-1849), Polish composer
and pianist, d. Paris

IT is a great error to imagine that the sensibil-
ities or the heart are blunted by a knowledge of musical science, or that our pleasures are
diminished by a refinement in musical taste ;
the imagination, on the contrary, in its exalted
flight on the pinions of wisdom, views art in a
world of ethereal beauty.   ANON.

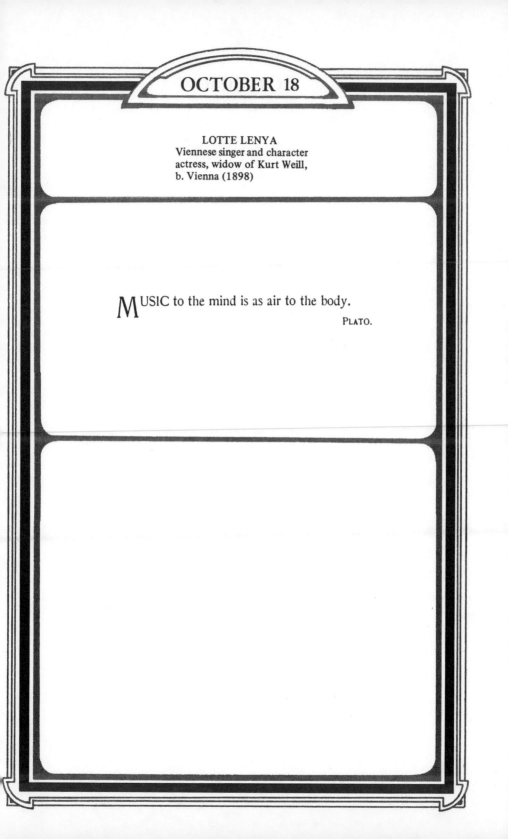

OCTOBER 18

LOTTE LENYA
Viennese singer and character
actress, widow of Kurt Weill,
b. Vienna (1898)

M USIC to the mind is as air to the body.

PLATO.

OCTOBER 19

First performance of Richard Wagner's
"Tannhäuser," Dresden (1845)

EVEN while I list, such music stealeth in upon
    my soul,
As though adown heaven's stair of stars the
seraph-harpings stole.

GERALD MASSY.

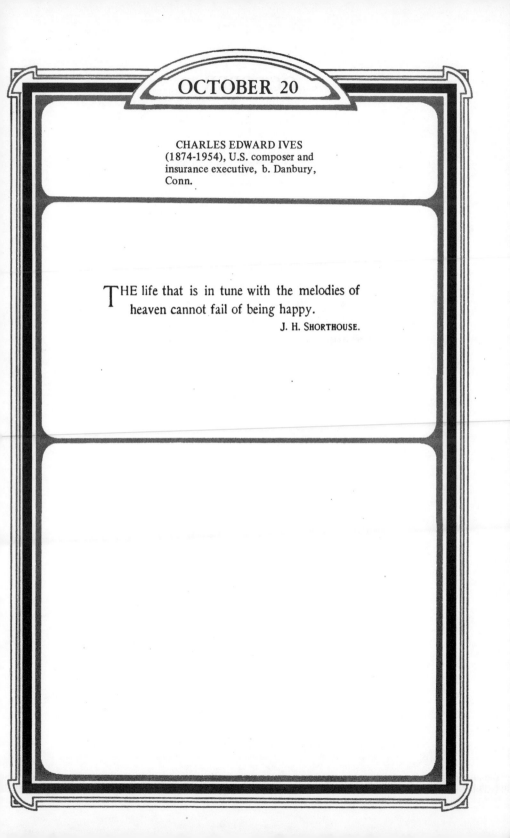

OCTOBER 20

CHARLES EDWARD IVES
(1874-1954), U.S. composer and
insurance executive, b. Danbury,
Conn.

THE life that is in tune with the melodies of
heaven cannot fail of being happy.

J. H. SHORTHOUSE.

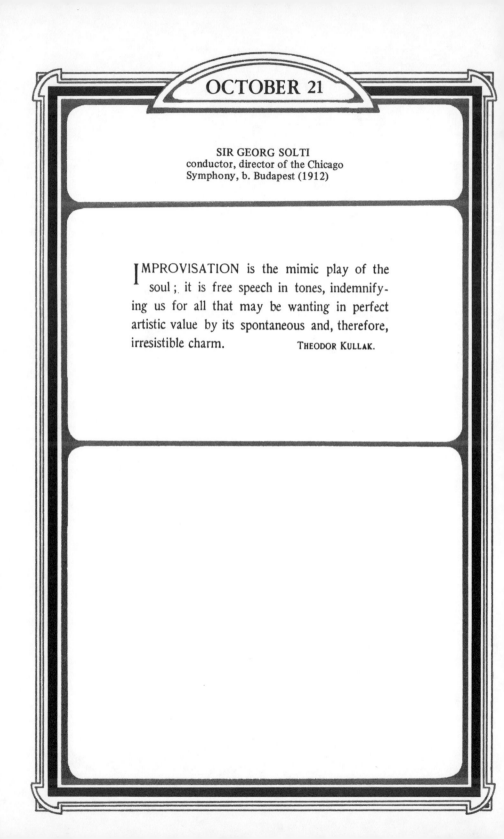

SIR GEORG SOLTI
conductor, director of the Chicago
Symphony, b. Budapest (1912)

IMPROVISATION is the mimic play of the soul; it is free speech in tones, indemnifying us for all that may be wanting in perfect artistic value by its spontaneous and, therefore, irresistible charm. THEODOR KULLAK.

FRANZ LISZT
(1811-1886), composer, pianist and
conductor, b. Raiding, Hungary

WOMEN are the music of life : they receive everything within themselves more openly and unconditionally than men, in order to beautify it with their sympathy.

WAGNER.

OCTOBER 23

Opening of the Metropolitan Opera House, New York City (1883), with a performance of Gounod's "Faust"

A MAN should hear a little music, read a little poetry, and see a fine picture every day of his life, in order that worldly cares may not obliterate the sense of the beautiful which God has implanted in the human soul.

GOETHE.

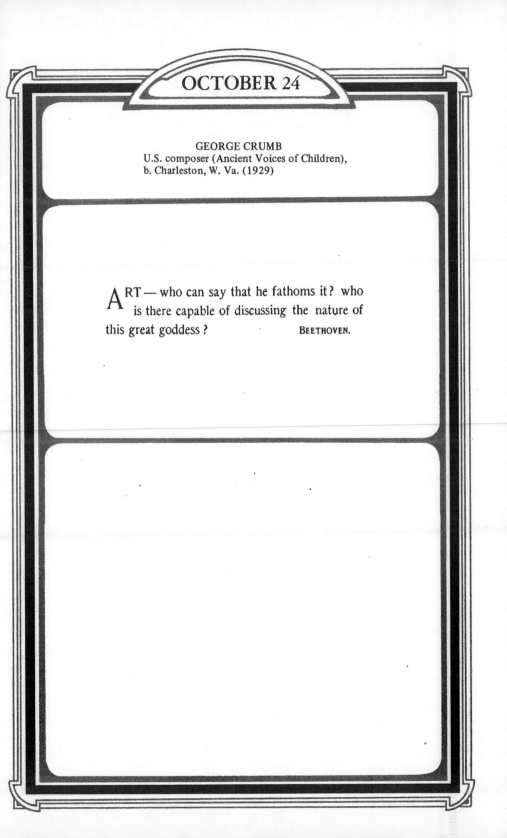

OCTOBER 24

GEORGE CRUMB
U.S. composer (Ancient Voices of Children),
b. Charleston, W. Va. (1929)

ART — who can say that he fathoms it? who is there capable of discussing the nature of this great goddess?   BEETHOVEN.

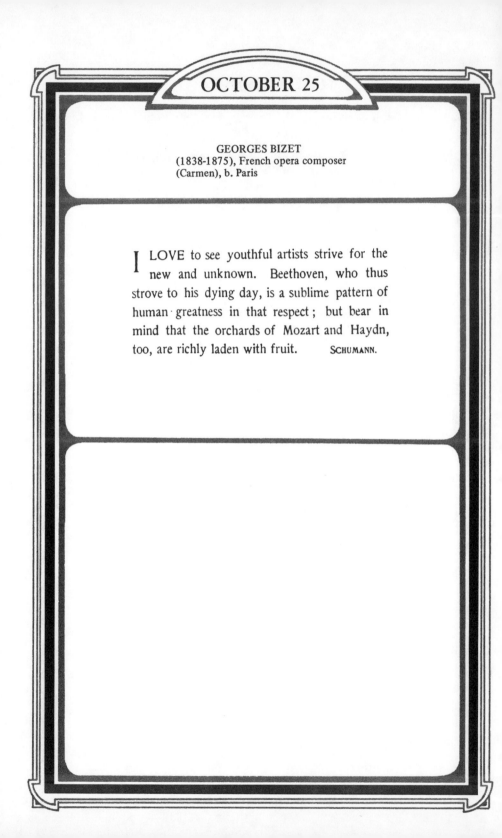

OCTOBER 25

GEORGES BIZET
(1838-1875), French opera composer
(Carmen), b. Paris

I LOVE to see youthful artists strive for the new and unknown. Beethoven, who thus strove to his dying day, is a sublime pattern of human greatness in that respect; but bear in mind that the orchards of Mozart and Haydn, too, are richly laden with fruit.   SCHUMANN.

OCTOBER 26

MAHALIA JACKSON
(1911-1972), U.S. gospel singer
and civil rights worker, b. New
Orleans

A S feeling is the alpha and omega of mind;
myth, that of history; lyrics, that of
poetry: so is the language of sounds the alpha
and omega of the language of words.

WAGNER.

OCTOBER 27

NICCOLÒ PAGANINI
(1782-1840), Italian virtuoso violinst
and composer, b. Genoa

TRAINING, cultivation, and enlightenment
are modifications of social life, results of
the industry and efforts of men toward improv-
ing their social condition.   MENDELSSOHN.

OCTOBER 28

HOWARD HANSON
U.S. composer, conductor, influental
teacher, b. Wahoo, Nebr. (1896)

IF I had to live my life again, I would have made it a rule to read some poetry and listen to some music at least once every week; for perhaps the part of my brain now atrophied would then have been kept active through use. The loss of these tastes is a loss of happiness, and may possibly be injurious to the intellect, and more probably to the moral character, by enfeebling the emotional part of our nature.

DARWIN.

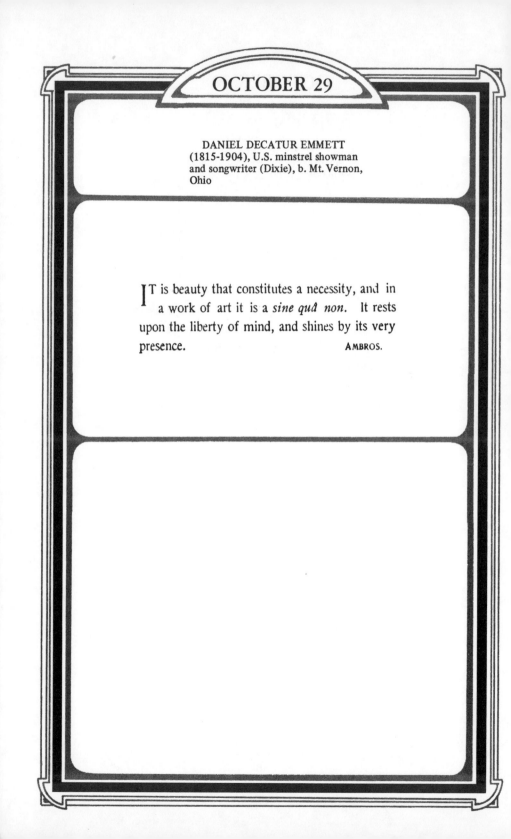

OCTOBER 29

DANIEL DECATUR EMMETT
(1815-1904), U.S. minstrel showman
and songwriter (Dixie), b. Mt. Vernon,
Ohio

IT is beauty that constitutes a necessity, and in a work of art it is a *sine quâ non*. It rests upon the liberty of mind, and shines by its very presence. AMBROS.

OCTOBER 30

First performance of Aaron Copland's Appalachian Spring," given by Martha Graham and her dance company, Washington, D.C. (1944)

I T is a powerful magnetic current that connects the two forms of human thought and feeling as expressed in poetry and music.   LISZT.

PHILIPPE DE VITRY
(1291-1361), French composer, poet, and influential
theorist, whose treatise, "Ars Nova," gave the musical
period its name, b. Vitry, Champagne

S O faith is strong
Only when we are strong, shrinks when
we shrink.
It comes when music stirs us, and the chords
Moving on some grand climax shake our souls
With influx new that makes new energies.
It comes in swellings of the heart and tears
That rise at noble and at gentle deeds.

GEORGE ELIOT.

HALLOWEEN

NOVEMBER

THANKSGIVING DAY

1979	November 22
1980	November 27
1981	November 26
1982	November 25
1983	November 24
1984	November 22
1985	November 28
1986	November 27
1987	November 26

ELECTION DAY: The first Tuesday after the first Monday

NOVEMBER 1

VICTORIA DE LOS ANGELES
Spanish soprano, b. Barcelona
(1923)

WHETHER music be expressive of joy, sensual or spiritual, the heart at least will understand it.

ANON.

NOVEMBER 2

GEORGE BERNARD SHAW
(1856 - 1950), dramatist and music critic
(under the name of "Corno de Bassetto"),
d. Syot St. Lawrence, England

M USIC alone has the inherent power of interpreting transcendent affections with
absolute truth.   FRANZ.

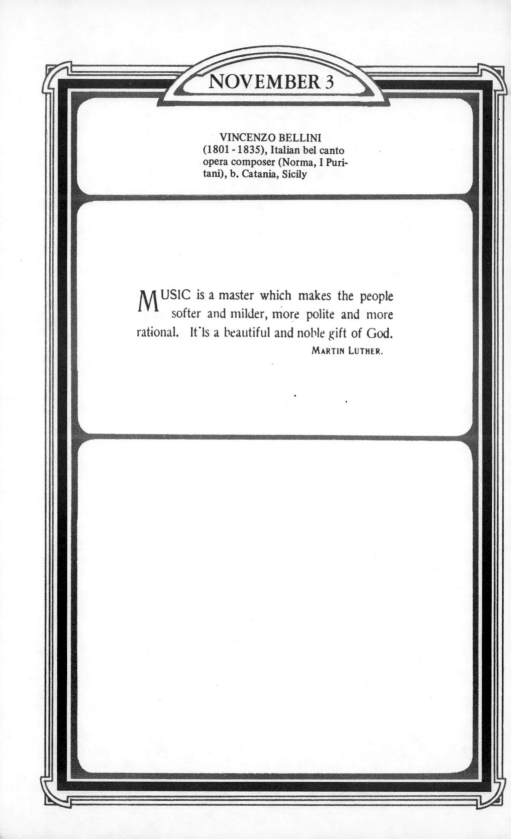

NOVEMBER 3

VINCENZO BELLINI
(1801 - 1835), Italian bel canto
opera composer (Norma, I Puri-
tani), b. Catania, Sicily

MUSIC is a master which makes the people softer and milder, more polite and more rational. It is a beautiful and noble gift of God.

MARTIN LUTHER.

NOVEMBER 4

First performance of Richard
Strauss's opera, "Intermezzo,"
Dresden (1924)

M USIC is the poetry of sounds.   But the
sound-waves from the tone-world are the
precursors of a future that we never shall see or
experience.   JEAN PAUL.

NOVEMBER 5

HANS SACHS
(1484-1576), German Meistersinger poet and composer, central figure in Richard Wagner's "Die Meistersinger," b. Nuremberg

L ET music sound while he doth make his choice;
Then, if he lose, he makes a swan-like end,
Fading in music.   SHAKESPEARE.

NOVEMBER 6

JOHN PHILIP SOUSA
(1854-1932), U.S. band leader
and march composer, b. Washington, D.C.

LESS than a God, they thought, there could
    not dwell
Within the hollow of that shell
That sung so sweetly and so well.   DRYDEN.

JOAN SUTHERLAND
Australian soprano, b.
Sydney (1926)

AND music, too — dear music! that can touch
Beyond all else the soul that loves it much —
Now heard far off, so far as but to seem
Like the faint, exquisite music of a dream.

MOORE.

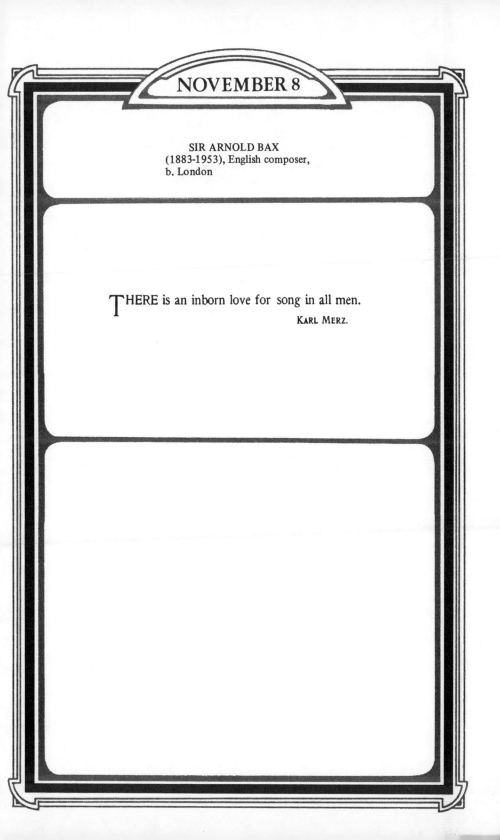

NOVEMBER 8

SIR ARNOLD BAX
(1883-1953), English composer,
b. London

T HERE is an inborn love for song in all men.

KARL MERZ.

NOVEMBER 9

First performance, in Barcelona of
"Boncierto de Aranjuez" for guitar
and orchestra by the blind Spanish
composer, Joaquín Rodrigo (1940)

IF we hearken to frivolous or insincere music,
we may extinguish the last light God has
left burning within us to lead the way to find
Him anew.   WAGNER.

NOVEMBER 10

First performance of Giuseppe
Verdi's "La Forza del Destino,"
St. Petersburg, Russia (1862)

POOR music expresses human sentiments but poorly; and for this reason it is bound to die before it goes very far. It comes not from the heart, hence it fails to go to the heart, and for this reason it lacks true life and must pass away. SCHOPENHAUER.

HOAGY CARMICHAEL
U.S. jazz pianist and composer,
b. Bloomington, Indiana (1899)

FOR the musician the eye does more than the ear, and the most intimate acquaintance with works of which they have never heard a note is, among musicians, as common as possible.

HULLAH.

NOVEMBER 12

ALEXANDER BORODIN
(1883-1887), Russian composer
(Prince Igor, Polovetsian Dances),
b. St. Petersburg

L ET there be no noise made, my gentle
    friends ;
Unless some dull and favorable hand
Will whisper music to my weary spirit.

SHAKESPEARE.

GEORGE WHITFIELD CHADWICK
(1854-1931), U.S. composer and teacher,
prominent member of the "Boston Classi-
cists" group, b. Lowell, Mass.

A ND like a bride of old in triumph led,
   With music and sweet showers,
Of festal flowers,
Unto the dwelling she must sway.

TENNYSON.

NOVEMBER 14

AARON COPLAND
U.S. composer, b. Brooklyn,
N.Y. (1900)

THE effect I expect from music is that it should excite and agitate me. Surely you do not imagine that I listen to music merely for the sake of pleasure ! BERLIOZ.

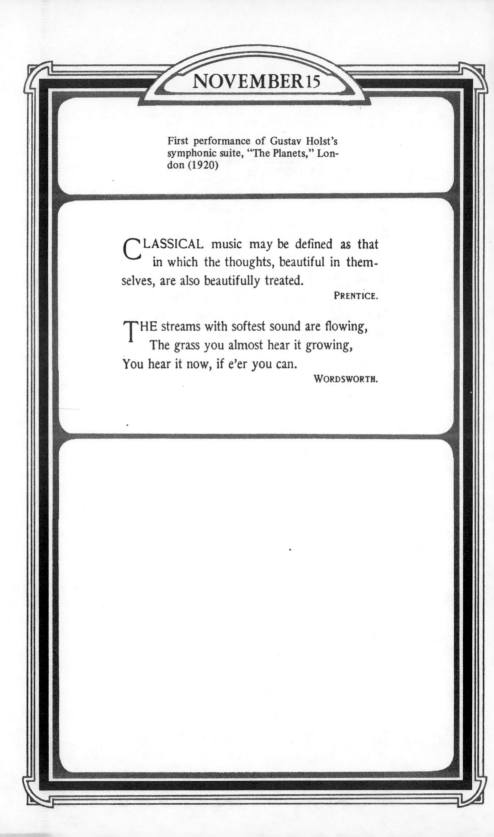

NOVEMBER 15

First performance of Gustav Holst's symphonic suite, "The Planets," London (1920)

CLASSICAL music may be defined as that in which the thoughts, beautiful in themselves, are also beautifully treated.

PRENTICE.

THE streams with softest sound are flowing,
  The grass you almost hear it growing,
You hear it now, if e'er you can.

WORDSWORTH.

NOVEMBER 16

PAUL HINDEMITH
(1895-1963), German-American
composer and eminent teacher,
b. Hanau

THE unsurpassable Bach knew a million times
more than all the rest of us put together.

SCHUMANN.

DAVID AMRAM
U.S. experimental composer,
b. Philadelphia (1930)

MUSIC is a heart-language; it is a heavenly language, and he who banishes heaven from his heart, fails also to fully comprehend the tone-language.   KARL MERZ.

NOVEMBER 18

EUGENE ORMANDY
U.S. conductor and director of the
Philadelphia Orchestra since 1938,
b. Bloomington, Indiana (1899)

L ET us accept music as a gift, a most precious gift of God; let us study it with reverence, let us practise it with humility and diligence, so that we may catch and drink in the spirit of love which it breathes, which is of God, and which leads to God.   KARL MERZ.

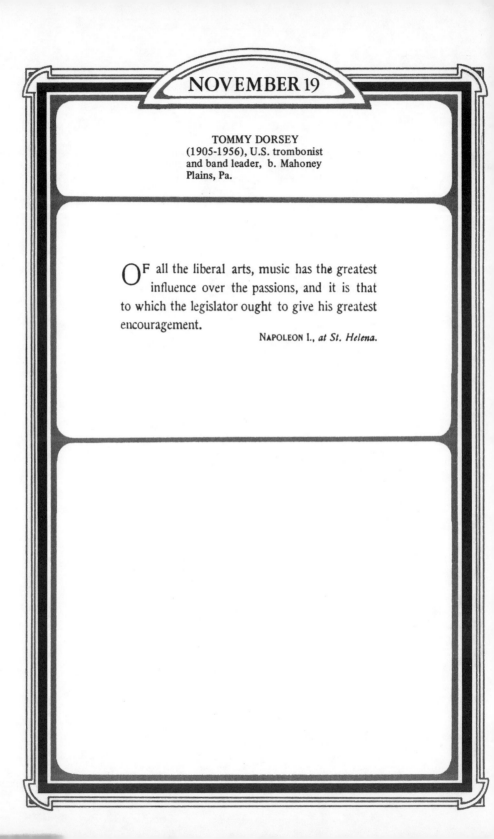

NOVEMBER 19

TOMMY DORSEY
(1905-1956), U.S. trombonist
and band leader, b. Mahoney
Plains, Pa.

OF all the liberal arts, music has the greatest
influence over the passions, and it is that
to which the legislator ought to give his greatest
encouragement.

NAPOLEON I., *at St. Helena.*

PIERRE DE LA RUE
(c.1460-1518), great Franco-Flemish composer and contemporary of Josquin de Prez, d. Courtrai

L ET the child of affliction take comfort in finding one like himself who, in spite of all the impediments of nature, yet did all that lay in his power to obtain admittance into the rank of worthy artists and men.   BEETHOVEN.

NOVEMBER 21

HENRY PURCELL
(c.1659-1695), English court
composer (Dido and Aeneas),
d. London

WHY my productions take from my hand
that particular form and style that makes
them Mozartish, and different from the works
of other composers, is probably owing to the
same cause which renders my nose so or so
large, so aquiline, or, in short, makes it
Mozart's, and different from those of other
people.   MOZART.

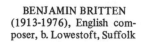

BENJAMIN BRITTEN
(1913-1976), English com-
poser, b. Lowestoft, Suffolk

MEN who divest music of its religious element, and claim to derive pleasure from
the art, are like galvanized frog-legs. There is
motion, but no life. There may be emotions,
but there is no love. AMBROS.

MANUEL DE FALLA
(1876-1946), Spanish
composer, b. Cadiz

M USIC is not a mere pastime. Its effects
are both powerful and beneficial, not only
upon the cultured few, but upon the uncultured
many.   HAWEIS.

SCOTT JOPLIN
(1868-1917), U.S. ragtime pianist
and composer, b. Texarkana

M USIC could be made the means to wean the
people from the low pleasures which bru-
talize and debase.   C. WILLEBY.

NOVEMBER 25

VIRGIL THOMSON
U.S. composer and critic, b.
Kansas City, Mo. (1896)

M USIC will give you whatever you are
capable of receiving. H. R. HAWEIS.

DAVID EWEN
prolific U.S. writer on music,
b. Lwow, Poland (1907)

OH Music! thou bringest the receding waves of eternity nearer to the weary soul of man as he stands upon the shore and longs to cross over! Art thou the evening of this life and the morning of the next?

J. P. RICHTER.

GUILLAUME DUFAY
(c.1400-1474), greatest of the early 15th-
century Burgundian composers, chief form-
ulator of the Renaissance musical style, d.
Cambrai

M USIC is a shower-bath of the soul, wash-
ing away all that is impure.

SCHOPENHAUER.

JEAN-BAPTISTE LULLY
(1682-1687), Italian-French composer
and conductor, founder of French opera,
b. Florence

M USIC is almost all we have of heaven on
earth.   ADDISON.

GAETANO DONIZETTI
(1797 - 1848), Italian opera composer
(Lucia de Lammermoor, Don Pasquale),
b. Bergamo

VERY few people realize the intense sacrificial devotion and tireless energy of an artist in music, who is high-priest in his art. It is work and work and work, and daily sacrifice for the benefit of mankind.   ANON.

NOVEMBER 30

ERNST EULENBERG
(1847-1926), German music
publisher, founder of the firm
of Ernst Eulenberg, Ltd., b.
Berlin

STUDY music in order to beautify your own heart, and beautify your own heart in order to make this world more beautiful for others.   ANON.

WAGNER'S BIRTHPLACE IN LEIPZIG

DECEMBER

DECEMBER 1

The first performance of Leonard Bernstein's musical, "Candide," New York, (1956)

THE Muse, though often persecuted, finds a home everywhere; did not Dædalus, when confined in the labyrinth, invent wings which carried him up into the air?   BEETHOVEN.

DECEMBER 2

SIR JOHN BARBIROLLI
(1899-1970), English conductor
and cellist, b. London

D EAR gentle Muse, whene'er by joy forsaken,
    And weary with the toils of life I sigh,
Thou dost my heart to love and hope awaken,
And point the way to brighter realms on high.

SCHOBER.

DECEMBER 3

MARIA CALLAS
(1923-1977), Greek-American
soprano, b. New York City

TRAINING in music is tantamount to discipline, and cannot be derived from that license which acknowledges no law except this — not to be bound by any law.   AMBROS.

DECEMBER 4

LIONEL HAMPTON
jazz vibraphonist, pianist
and band leader, b. Louisville, Ky. (1913)

MUSIC would not be inexpedient after meat, to assist and cherish Nature in her first concoction, and send the listeners' minds back to study in good tune.   MILTON.

DECEMBER 5

First performance of Hector Berlioz's
"Requiem," Paris (1837)

IT is only when our feelings, our mind, and our taste derive full satisfaction from music, that our pleasure in art really begins. Those who delight in mere concord of sounds are incapable of deeper appreciation.   FERDINAND HILLER.

DECEMBER 6

DAVE BRUBECK
U.S. jazz pianist and composer,
b. Concord, Calif. (1920)

M USIC is the lock and key to our memories
and our affections.   SCHOPENHAÙER.

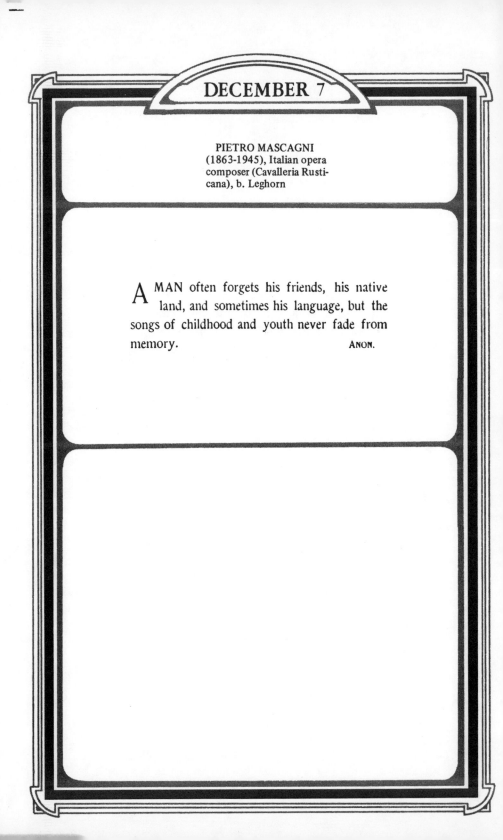

PIETRO MASCAGNI
(1863-1945), Italian opera
composer (Cavalleria Rusti-
cana), b. Leghorn

A MAN often forgets his friends, his native land, and sometimes his language, but the songs of childhood and youth never fade from memory. ANON.

DECEMBER 8

JAN SIBELIUS
(1865-1957), Finish composer,
b. Tavastehus

CORDS that vibrate sweetest pleasure
Breathe the deepest notes of woe.

BURNS.

DECEMBER 9

ELIZABETH SCHWARZKOPF
German soprano, b. near Poznan
(1915)

WHERE painting is weakest, — namely, in the expression of the highest moral and spiritual ideas, — there music is sublimely strong.   MRS. STOWE.

CÉSAR FRANCK
(1822-1890), Belgian composer
and organist, b. Liege

A DISTINGUISHED philosopher spoke of architecture as *frozen* music, and his assertion caused many to shake their heads. We believe this really beautiful idea could not be better reintroduced than by calling architecture *silent* music.   GOETHE.

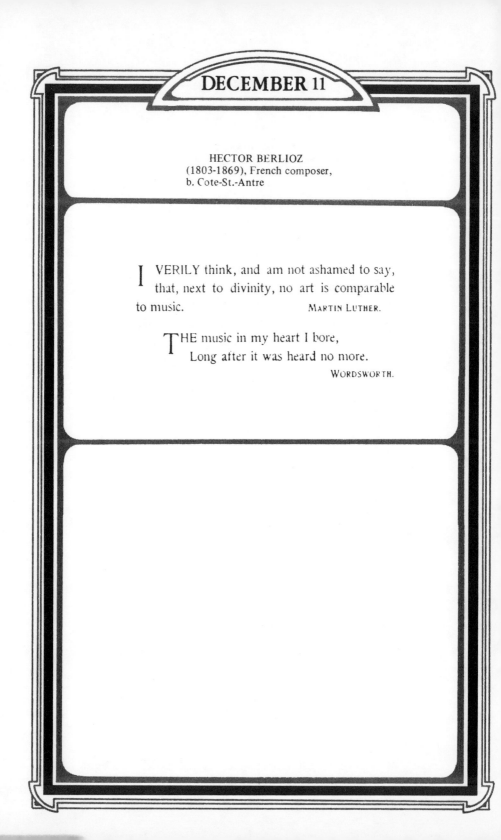

DECEMBER 11

HECTOR BERLIOZ
(1803-1869), French composer,
b. Cote-St.-Antre

I VERILY think, and am not ashamed to say,
that, next to divinity, no art is comparable
to music.   MARTIN LUTHER.

THE music in my heart I bore,
Long after it was heard no more.
                              WORDSWORTH.

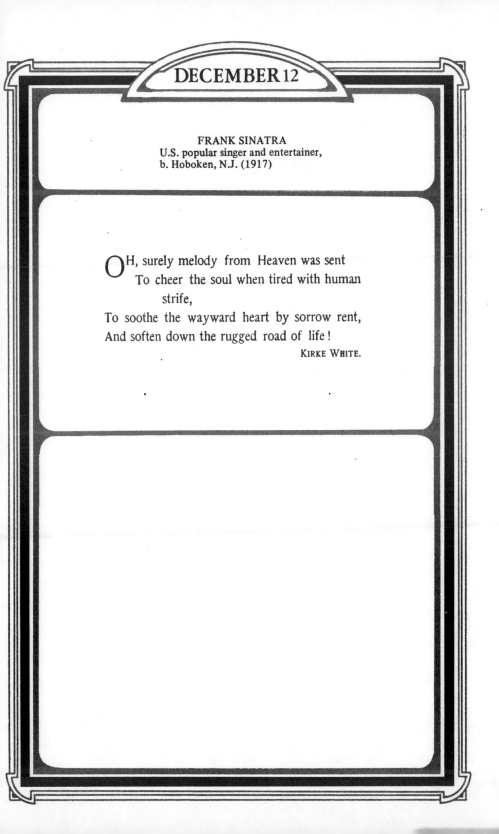

FRANK SINATRA
U.S. popular singer and entertainer,
b. Hoboken, N.J. (1917)

OH, surely melody from Heaven was sent
To cheer the soul when tired with human
strife,
To soothe the wayward heart by sorrow rent,
And soften down the rugged road of life!

KIRKE WHITE.

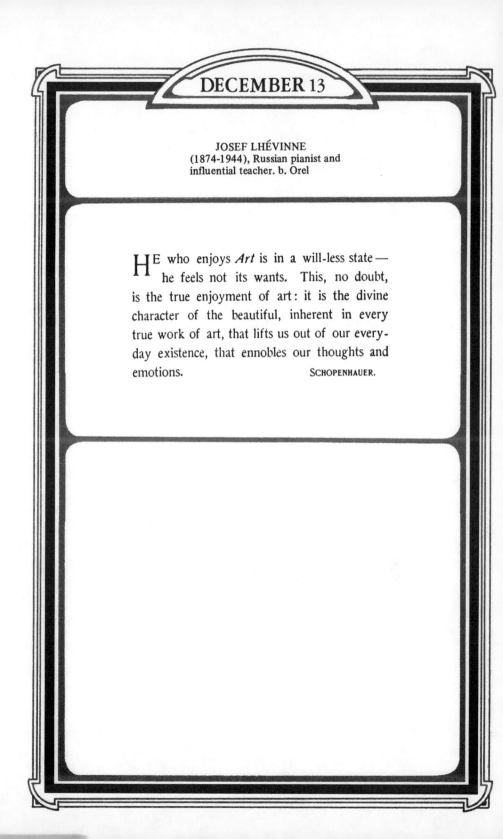

JOSEF LHÉVINNE
(1874-1944), Russian pianist and
influential teacher. b. Orel

HE who enjoys *Art* is in a will-less state — he feels not its wants. This, no doubt, is the true enjoyment of art: it is the divine character of the beautiful, inherent in every true work of art, that lifts us out of our everyday existence, that ennobles our thoughts and emotions.   SCHOPENHAUER.

ROSALYN TURECK
U.S. harpsichordist and pianist,
b. Chicago (1914)

THE better music is known and understood, the more it will be valued and esteemed: and a love of the higher school of musical composition is one of the surest tests of a refined and elegant state of society.   MOORE.

MICHEL-RICHARD DE LALANDE
(1657-1726), French court composer
to Louis XIV, b. Paris

TRUE Art brings us in contact with the divine idea, and in this sense all true *Art* must be sacred. · SCHOPENHAUER.

LUDWIG VAN BEETHOVEN
(1770-1827), German composer
and pianist, b. Bonn

NO important result can be attained with re-gard to the accomplishment of any object which affects the temporal or eternal well-being of our species, without enlisting an entire de-votedness to it of intelligence, zeal, fidelity, in-dustry, integrity, and practical exertion.

THOMAS H. GALLAUDET.

DECEMBER 17

ARTHUR FIEDLER
U.S. conductor, director of the
Boston Pops, b. Boston (1894)

L UDWIG VAN BEETHOVEN — " Yes, love
him, love him truly and sincerely — but do
not forget that he reached the goal of poetical
freedom only by the way of many years' ear-
nest and incessant study, and thus admire his
never-resting moral power."   SCHUMANN.

DECEMBER 18

ANTONIO STRADIVARI
(1644-1737), most celebrated
of the Italian violin makers, d.
Cremona

PASSION, whether great or not, must never
be expressed in an exaggerated manner, and
music — even in the most harrowing moment —
ought never to offend the ear, but should always
remain music, which desires to give pleasure.

MOZART.

DECEMBER 19

First performance of Gustav Mahler's unfinished
"Tenth Symphony" as realized by English musicologist Deryck Cooke, London (1960)

THERE 'S music in the dawning morn,
  There 's music in the twilight cloud,
There 's music in the depth of night,
When the world is still and dim,
And the stars flame out in the pomp of light,
Like thrones of the cherubim!

HONE : *Every-Day Book.*

DECEMBER 20

HENRY HADLEY
(1871-1937), U.S. composer and
conductor, b. Somerville, Mass.

M USIC religious heat inspires,
   It wakes the soul and lifts it high,
And wings it with sublime desires,
And fits it to bespeak the Deity.   ADDISON.

DECEMBER 21

MICHAEL TILSON THOMAS
U.S. conductor, b. Hollywood,
Calif. (1944)

M USIC is, so to speak, a disciplinarian as well as a mistress, making people kinder, gentler, more staid, and reasonable. Bad fiddlers and violinists show us what a fine art music really is, for white shows plainer in contrast to black. MARTIN LUTHER.

GIACOMO PUCCINI
(1858-1924), Italian opera
composer, b. Lucca

THE dignity of art perhaps chiefly manifests itself in music, as it contains no adventitious elements. Consisting chiefly in form and feeling, it brightens and refines whatever it expresses. ANON.

DECEMBER 23

ROSS LEE FINNEY
U.S. composer and teacher,
b. Wells, Minn. (1906)

M USIC is a beautiful and glorious gift of
God, the reflection of the heavenly harmonies in which His angels and all the celestial
host ever praise and glorify their Creator, singing in sweet strains: Holy, holy, holy, Lord
God of Sabaoth.   MICHAEL PRAETORIUS.

DECEMBER 24

JOHN DUNSTABLE
(c.1370-1453), astrologer, mathematician
and most important English composer of
the early 15th-century, d. London

M USIC revives the recollections it would
appease.   MADAME DE STAËL.

O F all the arts, great music is the art
To raise the soul above all earthly storms.
LELAND: *The Music-Lesson of Confucius.*

DECEMBER 25

First complete performance of Handel's "Messiah" in the U.S. given by the Handel and Haydn Society, Boston (1818)

IN an organ from one blast of wind
To many a row of pipes the sound-board
breathes.   MILTON: *Paradise Lost.*

MEN, even when alone, lighten their labors
by song, however rude it may be.
                                    QUINTILIAN.

DECEMBER 26

First performance of Vincenzo Bellini's
"Norma," La Scala, Milan (1831)

THE life of music flows onward in melody, or
in various melodies side by side; it is important, above all, to preserve this life undis-
turbed and unadulterated in its flow, and in its
entirety — just as it is the first duty of man to
be, above all, true to himself and to his calling.

A. B. MARX.

DECEMBER 27

PHILLIP SPITTA
(1841 - 1894), German musicologist
and eminent Bach scholar, b. Hanover

AS the love of God is immeasurably great,
so no one has as yet fathomed the depth
of music. It is the love-language of the soul;
it is the medium between this and the other
world, between the natural and supernatural.

ANON.

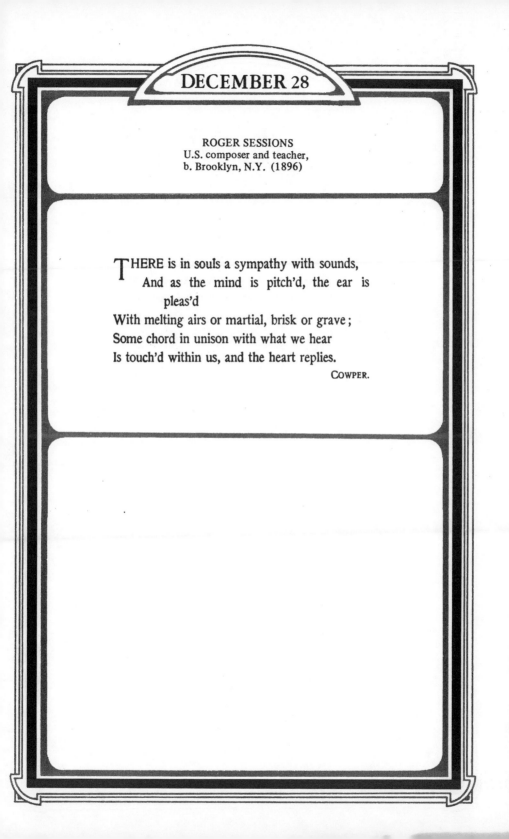

DECEMBER 28

ROGER SESSIONS
U.S. composer and teacher,
b. Brooklyn, N.Y. (1896)

THERE is in souls a sympathy with sounds,
    And as the mind is pitch'd, the ear is
        pleas'd
With melting airs or martial, brisk or grave;
Some chord in unison with what we hear
Is touch'd within us, and the heart replies.

COWPER.

DECEMBER 29

PABLO CASALS
(1876-1973), Spanish cellist
and conductor, b. Vendrell,
Catalonia

THE struggle through which a musician has to pass, cannot be regarded as a very great hardship: if music is not his natural calling, he will give it up for want of success; but if he is a favorite of the Muse, he will triumph in spite of it.   HAUPTMANN.

First performance of Sergei Prokofiev's opera,
"The Love for Three Oranges," under the composer's direction, Chicago (1921)

MUSIC remains the universal language of nature; it speaks to us in wonderful and mysterious tones; in vain do we try to retain its effect by signs, for any artificial connecting of the hieroglyphs results after all only in indicating the idea of that which we have heard.

E. T. A. HOFFMANN.

DECEMBER 31

JULE STYNE
U.S. songwriter and composer of stage
musicals (Gypsy, Gentlemen Prefer
Blondes), b. London (1905)

THE beautiful can have but one source, it can
be concentrated in but one being, and this
is none other than God.   SCHOPENHAUER.

NEW YEAR'S EVE